The Conscious Evolution: Reinterpreting Adam Through Science and Revelation

Harsa khan

Published by Harsa khan, 2025.

Table of Contents

To every seeker of truth—who dared to question,who refused blind belief,who chose reason over ritual,and who walked the lonely path of understandingwith nothing but honesty and conscience as light.

"We will show them Our signs in the universe and within themselves, until it becomes clear to them that this is the Truth."

— Qur'an, Surah Fussilat (41:53)

Author's Preface

Title: *The Conscious Evolution: Reinterpreting Adam Through Science and Revelation*

The story of Adam has long been confined to myth, metaphor, or rigid literalism. For generations, we have inherited interpretations shaped by political power, mystical folklore, and uncritical acceptance. But what if the truth about Adam was never meant to be a fairy tale of clay and sin, nor a divine puppet's fall from paradise, but rather a grand evolutionary and intellectual awakening of human consciousness?

This book is the result of years of interdisciplinary exploration—across Quranic linguistics, neuroscience, embryology, evolutionary biology, and the science of consciousness. Here, I present a new framework: one where Adam is neither just an individual nor merely symbolic, but the embodiment of the rise of moral, cognitive, and social awareness in human beings. This is not just a reinterpretation—it is a reclamation of human dignity through the lens of science and divine revelation, without the burden of inherited distortions.

I write this book not as a religious scholar, but as a seeker—guided by reason, evidence, and a deep reverence for the Quran as a book of consciousness and justice. Throughout this journey, I challenge traditional translations, expose mythologized dogmas, and illuminate verses that speak not to blind faith but to rational awakening.

This work is for those unafraid to ask:

What if Adam was not the first man—but the first *mind*?

– Harsa Khan

Index:

Chapter 1: Who Was Adam – Symbol or Man?

Introduction: A Critical Question

The story of *Adam* is among the most frequently mentioned and yet most misunderstood narratives in the Quran. Across religious traditions, Adam is often imagined as the "first man" molded from clay, placed in a heavenly garden, and later expelled due to disobedience. But the Quran's message is fundamentally different from traditional interpretations built around mythological and dogmatic beliefs. This chapter seeks to peel away centuries of distortion and re-examine Adam not as a physical individual, but as a **symbolic emergence of self-aware, morally conscious humanity**.

This exploration will rely purely on the Quranic language, supported by findings in psychology, neuroscience, anthropology, and evolutionary biology. The question is not whether Adam existed in flesh and blood, but **what Adam represents**, and **why** the Quran made him central to the narrative of human dignity, error, and evolution.

The Quran Does Not Say Adam Was the First Biological Human

Contrary to common belief, the Quran never explicitly says Adam was the **first biological man**. The text only states that Allah created the human being from **clay**, and that **Adam was taught names**, disobeyed, felt regret, and was guided.

There is no verse in the Quran that declares: *"Adam was the first human created among all species and all other human-like forms were absent."*

Instead, the Quran uses **symbolic language** to show:

- Clay (teen) represents **material origin**.
- Nafakh (breathing of spirit) symbolizes **activation of consciousness**.
- Names taught to Adam symbolize **mental categorization, abstraction, and language**—a profound neurological leap.

Thus, *Adam* in the Quran is not the beginning of biology, but the **awakening of cognition and conscience.**

Adam Is Taught "Names" – What Does That Mean?

The most crucial verse about Adam is:

> *"And He taught Adam all the names..."*
>
> (Surah Al-Baqarah 2:31)

This verse is central. Names here don't refer to "Tom, Dick, and Harry." The Arabic word **"Asmaa"** refers to *attributes, concepts, and identifiers*. This implies:

- **Language acquisition**: The ability to link words with abstract meanings.
- **Cognitive categorization**: To divide the world into ideas, relationships, and meaning systems.
- **Self-awareness**: Recognizing one's own role, responsibility, and limits.

Modern neuroscience confirms that the **prefrontal cortex** in the human brain is responsible for planning, decision-making, language, and moral reasoning. What the Quran describes as being "taught names" matches precisely the **evolutionary leap** in hominids that led to the rise of *Homo sapiens* as a distinct form of intelligent life.

Thus, the "teaching of names" is the Quran's way of saying that **Adam is the birth of conscious, ethical, linguistic humanity.** Not necessarily a singular male individual, but a **stage in the evolutionary development of intelligent life**.

The Story of Adam Is Not About Sin—It's About Choice

In classical religious thought, Adam is blamed for the "original sin," but the Quran refutes this concept. Instead, it presents Adam as:

- A being capable of making **mistakes**.
- One who experiences **regret**.
- One who receives **guidance**, not punishment.

"Then Adam received words from his Lord, so He turned to him in mercy. Indeed, He is the Accepting of repentance, the Merciful."

(Surah Al-Baqarah 2:37)

This is not a story of damnation. It is a story of **moral evolution**. Adam disobeys, but then he uses his *Qalb* (inner consciousness), feels regret, and reforms. That moment is when *Adam becomes truly human*—capable of error but also capable of learning.

Thus, Adam represents the emergence of **free will**, **emotional depth**, and **the capacity to evolve beyond instinct**.

Adam and the Shajr: Symbolism, Not Myth

The famous story of Adam eating from the forbidden tree is not about a literal fruit or a literal tree. It is **symbolic**:

- The "tree" represents **forbidden knowledge**—the understanding of duality (good/evil), temptation, and desire.
- Eating from it symbolizes the **use of free will**, stepping into **independent ethical consciousness**.
- Adam's "descent" from the garden represents **transition from innocence to experience**.

This symbolism matches what happens in human psychological development. A child is innocent, living in a protected world (symbolic *Jannat*). But as awareness develops, the child becomes responsible, aware of consequences. This transition is **not a fall**, but a **rise in consciousness**—a core theme of the Quranic Adam story.

Adam vs. Angels: Intellect vs. Programming

In Surah Al-Baqarah, God says:

> *"I know what you do not know."* (2:30)

And the angels say:

> *"Will You place in it one who causes corruption and sheds blood?"*

Here, the angels represent **instinctive programming**—they follow without choice.

Adam, by contrast, is taught names—he represents **learning, change, and ethical growth**. He can choose, err, and recover.

This shows that **Adam symbolizes the superiority of conscious, evolving intelligence over blind obedience**. The Quran praises not passive worship, but **self-aware moral agency**.

Adam Was Not a Jew, Christian, or Muslim

> *"Abraham was neither a Jew nor a Christian, but upright and submitted to God."*
>
> (Surah Aali-Imran 3:67)

Likewise, Adam predates all religions and sects. He cannot be claimed by any religious group. He represents **universal human potential**—free of dogma.

To reclaim Adam is to **reclaim humanity from religious ownership**. His story belongs to all, not to clerics, theologians, or sects.

Conclusion: Adam Is Every Human Who Wakes Up

The Quran's purpose is not to tell bedtime stories. It is to awaken human consciousness. Adam is a symbol of that awakening.

- He represents the **rise of intelligence over instinct**.

- He reflects the **pain of error and the power of repentance**.
- He is not our shame. He is our **mirror**.

Whenever a human reflects, questions, learns, and transforms, they are **repeating the journey of Adam**. He is not one man of the past. He is the **story of all of us.**

> *"Indeed, We have honored the children of Adam..."*
>
> (Surah Al-Isra 17:70)

That honor comes not from rituals or robes, but from **reason, choice, emotion, and action.**

Let us reclaim Adam—not as a mythical first man, but as the **first call to awaken the human potential buried within each of us**.

Chapter 2: Creation or Evolution? Quran's Middle Path

The ongoing debate between creationism and evolution has polarized scientific and religious communities for over a century. Creationists hold that God created humans instantly in their final form, while proponents of Darwinian evolution argue that life emerged through a slow, unguided process of natural selection. The Quran, however, introduces a third narrative—one of layered emergence, guided development, and inherent purpose. It neither clings to mythological literalism nor surrenders to atheistic materialism. This chapter explores how the Quranic worldview provides a middle path, harmonizing modern science with divine wisdom through a rational and spiritually enriched lens.

The False Binary: Creationism vs. Evolution

The traditional binary between creationism and evolution is flawed because it frames the question as either/or: either man was created instantly in his final form, or he is purely the result of random mutations. Both positions contain limitations:

- **Creationism** dismisses the abundant fossil record, genetic evidence, and embryological patterns linking all life forms.
- **Mainstream Evolutionary Theory** focuses solely on material mechanisms, often dismissing the metaphysical or purposive dimensions of life.

The Quran proposes neither of these extremes. It suggests that human life was formed through a sequence of deliberate, ordered stages, fully compatible with scientific discoveries yet grounded in divine purpose.

What Science Says About Evolution

Evolutionary biology describes the emergence of species through mechanisms such as:

- **Mutation**: Random alterations in DNA.
- **Natural Selection**: Favoring traits that enhance survival.
- **Genetic Drift and Gene Flow**: Genetic variation and recombination across populations.

The scientific method excels in explaining "how" these processes occur. However, it remains silent on deeper questions like:

- Why did life evolve toward increasing complexity?
- What is the origin of self-awareness and morality?
- Is consciousness reducible to neural chemistry?

These questions open a space where science and revelation may complement rather than contradict each other.

Gradual Creation in the Quran

Unlike the sudden creation narrative found in other scriptures, the Quran presents human origin as a process:

> "He created you in stages (atwara)." (Surah Nuh 71:14)
>
> "And certainly, did We create man from an extract of clay. Then We placed him as a drop in a firm lodging." (Surah Al-Mu'minun 23:12–13)

These verses highlight sequential development: from clay (earthly elements) to a drop (zygote), to a clinging clot, and so forth. The Quranic language inherently supports biological progression, showing consistency with embryology and evolutionary principles.

Linguistic Roots: The Word "Khalaqa"

The Arabic word **khalaqa** (create) does not imply instant magic; it denotes a measured, purposeful act. Quran uses multiple verbs for creation:

- **Khalaqa** – to proportion, to measure out.

- **Ansha'a** – to raise gradually.
- **Sawwara** – to shape or fashion.

Each of these reflects deliberate design over time, not spontaneous conjuration. This is linguistically aligned with the scientific concept of progressive development.

Adam: The Moment of Conscious Emergence

If we accept that Homo sapiens evolved over time, the question becomes: at what point did Adam appear? The Quran implies that Adam's uniqueness was not in biology but in **conscious self-awareness** and **moral responsibility**:

> "And when I have fashioned him and breathed into him of My Spirit, fall down before him in submission." (Surah Al-Hijr 15:29)

The infusion of "Ruh" signifies the emergence of consciousness, free will, ethical reasoning—elements that transcend biology. This can be interpreted as the point where evolving hominins became fully human.

Evolution with Divine Direction

Modern science is beginning to uncover patterns that suggest complexity and order, not randomness. Fields such as:

- **Epigenetics** show environmental impact on gene expression.
- **Systems biology** uncovers holistic patterns beyond isolated mutations.
- **Quantum biology** explores the influence of consciousness on biological functions.

These may be seen as reflections of divine programming—a universe unfolding through deterministic laws under a conscious will. The Quran emphasizes this:

> "Who perfected everything He created and began the creation of man from clay." (Surah As-Sajda 32:7)

Evolution of Consciousness: A Spiritual Trajectory

Evolution in the Quran is not merely about the physical form but the **ascent of consciousness.** From the inanimate to the sentient, and finally to the morally aware, the Quran traces a journey:

> "Was there not a period of time when man was nothing to be mentioned?" (Surah Al-Insan 76:1)
>
> "Then He made him hear and see." (Surah Al-Insan 76:2)
>
> "And guided him to the path." (Surah Al-Insan 76:3)

These stages mirror both embryological and evolutionary development and culminate in the moral agent—the Quranic Adam.

Reconciling Revelation and Reason

The Quran does not fear science. Instead, it urges observation, reflection, and rationality:

> "Do they not reflect upon their own selves?" (Surah Ar-Rum 30:8)
>
> "We will show them Our signs in the horizons and within themselves until it becomes clear to them that it is the truth." (Surah Fussilat 41:53)

Rather than conflict, the Quranic invitation is to see divine signs in the very mechanisms of biology, evolution, and cosmic order. The text accommodates science without surrendering to reductionism.

Conclusion: Quran's Middle Path

Creation and evolution need not be adversaries. The Quran proposes a developmental model guided by divine wisdom. Human beings evolved in physical form, but the advent of Adam marks the awakening of moral consciousness. This is not the abandonment of faith but its evolution—a call to reclaim religion as a path of inquiry, reason, and inner elevation. The Quranic Adam is not in conflict with science but completes what science begins.

Chapter 3: The Clay Code — Scientific Meaning of "Teen" in the Quran

Among the most repeated symbolic elements in the Quran's narrative of human origin is the mention of clay — specifically the term *Teen* (طِين). Unlike mythological representations of creation where man is molded like pottery from literal mud, the Quranic use of *Teen* is metaphorical, linguistic, and deeply aligned with scientific understandings of life's biochemical basis. This chapter explores the meaning of *Teen* in the Quran, its connection to the Earth's elements, and how modern chemistry and biology confirm this insight.

Quranic Terms for Earthly Origin

The Quran uses multiple Arabic terms to describe the material origin of the first human:

- **Teen** (— (طِينCommonly translated as clay.
- **Salsaal** (— (صَلْصَالٍHard clay, possibly baked or resonant like pottery.
- **Hama'in Masnun** (— (حَمَإٍ مَّسْنُونٍDark, stinky mud or decaying matter.
- **Turab** (— (تُرَابٍDust or soil.

Each term highlights a different stage or symbolic aspect of material transformation, suggesting an evolving biochemical process rather than a literal clay sculpture. The choice of these varied words is deliberate and aligned with Earth's biological history.

The Biochemical Reality: Carbon and the Elements of Life

Life on Earth is carbon-based. Human bodies, like all other known life forms, are composed primarily of elements found in Earth's crust and surface:

- **Carbon (C)**: Central to all organic molecules.
- **Hydrogen (H), Oxygen (O), Nitrogen (N)**: Found in proteins, carbohydrates, and DNA.

- **Calcium (Ca), Phosphorus (P), Sulfur (S), Iron (Fe), Potassium (K)**: Crucial for bones, enzymes, blood, and cellular function.

These elements are all abundantly present in soil, clay, and organic mud. Thus, when the Quran says that Adam was created from *teen*, it is scientifically sound to interpret it as the Earth-based biochemical composition of life — not as literal sculpture.

Teen as Symbol of Earthly Origin and Evolution

Clay is not just soil and water — it is a chemically active medium. It has the following properties that make it significant in origin-of-life theories:

- **Catalytic surfaces**: Clay can catalyze reactions necessary for forming RNA and amino acids.
- **Ionic charges**: These help in organizing molecules, potentially assisting in the polymerization of organic compounds.
- **Preservation**: Clay can encapsulate molecules, protecting them from decay.

In this sense, *Teen* is a metaphor not just for raw material, but for Earth's ability to produce complex biological systems — a fitting poetic description for the emergence of life.

Quranic Consistency: From Dust to Development

Consider this verse:

> "He created him from clay like [that of] pottery." — **Quran 55:14**
>
> "Indeed, We created you from dust..." — **Quran 22:5**
>
> "And We created man from an extract of clay (sulaalah min teen)." — **Quran 23:12**

The progression in these verses mirrors developmental biology:

- *Turab* (dust): Basic mineral particles.
- *Teen* (clay): Moist, active Earth mixture.
- *Sulaalah min Teen*: Extract of clay, hinting at the purified, bioactive chemical composition used for life.
- *Salsaal*: Dried or matured form, potentially representing the formed biological body.

Thus, Quranic language reveals stages from elemental origin to organic complexity, consistent with evolutionary biology and Earth science.

Linguistic Root Analysis: Teen (طِين))

The root word *ṭā-yā-nūn (ط ي ن)* in Arabic conveys a sense of mixing softness, stickiness, and potentiality. It is used to describe something that is:

- Pliable
- Rich in water
- Suitable for transformation

This fits the metaphor of clay as a dynamic matrix from which complex organisms can evolve. In ancient times, this observation was intuitive. But today, the linguistic depth and scientific accuracy of this metaphor are clearer than ever.

Scientific Theories: Clay Hypothesis in Origin of Life

Modern science explores the **Clay Hypothesis**, first proposed by A.G. Cairns-Smith. According to this theory:

- **Clay crystals** can form ordered layers which can encode and replicate information.
- These surfaces may have acted as templates for the formation of **RNA** — the building blocks of life.

Quranic use of *Teen* aligns surprisingly with this hypothesis. The Quran never describes a divine hand shaping a man like pottery but speaks in abstract, layered metaphors — in harmony with science.

The Metaphysical Aspect: Clay and Consciousness

Clay is lifeless, yet full of potential. Quran presents a dual concept:

- Material origin: *Teen*
- Conscious breath: *Ruh*

Together, they form the physical and metaphysical essence of humans. This shows a balanced worldview — acknowledging the biological and chemical origins while recognizing consciousness as an emergent, possibly quantum phenomenon (explored in the next chapter).

Rejecting Literalism: From Folklore to Forensics

Literal interpretations — such as imagining a God-like figure shaping clay statues — are influenced by Judeo-Christian mythologies. The Quran is more abstract, precise, and metaphorical.

- **It never mentions Hawwa (Eve) being made from Adam's rib.**
- **It never mentions literal sculpting.**
- **It never names clay as permanent material — it always transitions into biological processes.**

This sophistication invites deeper reflection — not myths but meaningful metaphors.

Conclusion: Clay as Code, Not Sculpture

The term *Teen* in the Quran represents Earth's rich chemical potential, not just mud. It symbolizes a stage in the natural evolution of life where inert matter began organizing into living, conscious beings. From a Quranic, scientific, and logical perspective, Adam's creation from *Teen* is not a magical event but a poetic reference to biochemical reality.

This understanding moves us away from myth and toward a rational appreciation of our origins — a necessary step for reconciling faith with reason.

Chapter 4: From Drop to Consciousness – The Stages of Human Development in the Womb

The Quran's description of the human formation inside the womb is both poetic and surprisingly accurate when read through the lens of embryology. The journey from a single microscopic drop to a fully formed, conscious being is not merely a biological process—it is the unfolding of nature's finest code. This chapter explores how Quranic verses align with modern science, especially embryology, and how they subtly point to a recurring design or "blueprint" that connects every human back to the archetype—Adam.

Quranic Terminology of Human Embryogenesis

The Quran repeatedly uses a set of specific terms to describe stages of human formation:

- **Nutfah** (نُطْفَةٍ) – The drop of fluid (sperm/zygote)
- **Alaqah** (عَلَقَةٍ) – A clinging substance, sometimes interpreted as a clot or leech-like entity
- **Mudghah** (مُضْغَةٍ) – A chewed-like lump of flesh
- **Izam** (عِظَامًا) – Bones
- **Lahm** (لَحْمًا) – Flesh/clothing of the bones

Surah Al-Mu'minun (23:12–14):

> "And certainly, We created man from an extract of clay. Then We made him a drop in a safe place. Then We created the drop into a clinging substance, then We made the clinging substance into a lump, then We made the lump bones, then We clothed the bones with flesh; then We developed him into another creation. So blessed is Allah, the best of creators."

Modern embryology confirms these stages almost sequentially. A zygote forms, implants in the uterus (clings), becomes a shaped structure (like chewed flesh), bones begin to form, and muscle tissue follows. Yet the most striking element is the closing line: **"then We developed him into another creation"**—a subtle pointer to consciousness, self-awareness, and individuality.

Nutfah: The Drop That Held a Universe

The word *Nutfah* is used over a dozen times in the Quran, pointing to the miraculous nature of a microscopic fluid carrying all the potential of a human being. In modern biology, we know that a sperm carries 23 chromosomes that combine with 23 from the egg to form a 46-chromosome zygote—containing the entire genetic instruction set.

This isn't merely a poetic choice. The word "*ma'in daafiq*" (gushing fluid) in Surah Tariq (86:6-7) further deepens this link. This divine emphasis on the smallest unit aligns with the scientific discovery that *DNA*—the microscopic helix—is the master template of life.

Alaqah and Mudghah: Embryonic Evolution in Visual Detail

- **Alaqah**, often mistranslated as a blood clot, actually aligns more with the meaning of something that clings or adheres—perfectly describing the embryo's implantation in the uterine wall.
- **Mudghah**, a chewed-like lump, matches the somite stage in embryology where the embryo appears segmented—similar to teeth marks on a piece of gum.

These visual metaphors are remarkable, especially given that such descriptions came centuries before the invention of the microscope.

Bones, Muscles, and the Transformation into "Another Creation"

The verse doesn't stop at mere anatomy. It explicitly divides the formation of bones and their subsequent covering with flesh. This anatomical accuracy is astonishing: bones (ossification centers) form first, and muscles (myogenesis) envelop them.

The phrase "then We made him into another creation" (*thumma ansha'naahu khalqan aakhar*) is where biology meets metaphysics. After the physical structure is complete, something intangible arrives—**consciousness.**

The Spark of Ruh: Is Consciousness a Later Phase?

Surah Al-Hijr (15:29) says:

> "So when I have proportioned him and breathed into him of My Spirit (Ruh), then fall down to him in prostration."

Here, the divine breath—*Ruh*—is not a physical act but a metaphor for the emergence of **conscious awareness, perception, will, and selfhood**. This occurs after the biological shell is completed. Neuroscience today suggests that **consciousness emerges from neural complexity** in later stages of brain development—again, consistent with the Quranic sequence.

This also refutes traditional mythologies of Ruh as a magical "soul." Instead, it presents a functional, scientific, and metaphysical emergence of the self.

The Womb as the Original Laboratory

The womb is portrayed in the Quran as a **"qarar makeen" (safe dwelling)** (Surah Al-Mu'minun 23:13). It is here that nature performs its most complex experiment—replicating Adam's design in every child. Every embryonic journey is a mini-replay of humanity's evolutionary and spiritual history.

Through this lens, **each human is an echo of Adam**—not biologically, but structurally, cognitively, and morally.

The Role of Time: From 40 to 120 Days?

Traditional hadith literature mentions stages occurring every 40 days, culminating in the infusion of Ruh at 120 days. However, this view is based on narrations, not the Quran itself. The Quran gives no such timeframe, suggesting a continuous process rather than a fixed day for consciousness.

Furthermore, neuroscientific studies show that significant brain development—and potential for self-awareness—does not emerge until the later trimesters, consistent with the Quran's nuanced, stage-wise approach.

Conclusion: Adamic Blueprint in Every Womb

Human development in the womb is not just biology—it's a philosophical reenactment of human consciousness emerging from clay and drop. It is where science meets the sacred. Every fetus undergoes a transformation from inert matter to living thought—a journey that reflects the Quranic Adam: a being rising from matter into mind, and from mind into moral choice.

Thus, the womb is not just a place of growth. It is the **first school of creation**, the cradle of consciousness, and the echo of Adam's origin. Every child born is a new chapter of the ancient story—retold through biology, evolved through time, and revealed through divine signs.

Chapter 5: Ruh — Breath of Consciousness or Superstition?

The concept of *Ruh* (روح) in the Quran is often misunderstood and misrepresented. Traditional interpretations associate it with a mystical or ghost-like "soul" that enters and exits the body. However, a deeper linguistic, logical, and scientific analysis presents *Ruh* not as an abstract supernatural entity but as a symbol of conscious awareness — a spark of Universal Consciousness. This chapter delves into the Quranic portrayal of *Ruh*, explores its semantic roots, and connects it to emerging insights from neuroscience and quantum consciousness.

The Linguistic Root of "Ruh"

The Arabic word *Ruh* comes from the root ر-و-ح (r-w-ḥ), which broadly refers to breath, wind, and movement. It shares the same root with *reha* (relief), *rauh* (comfort), and *reih* (fragrance or essence). This root indicates something that moves invisibly yet pervades and affects deeply. Thus, *Ruh* is more akin to a vital flow or essence — something that animates or enables awareness — not something physically separable from the body.

Quran does not describe *Ruh* as a ghost or shadowy figure. It says:

> **"They ask you about the Ruh. Say: The Ruh is from the command (amr) of my Lord..."** *(Quran 17:85)*

The word *amr* (أمر) here implies a direct action, will, or system-command — suggesting that *Ruh* is a functional, universal process rather than a mystical object.

Ruh as Universal Consciousness

Modern physics and neuroscience provide a new lens through which *Ruh* can be interpreted. Quantum biology and theories of consciousness now suggest that awareness is not just a product of brain chemistry but may be linked to an underlying informational field in the universe.

This perspective aligns remarkably with the Quran's portrayal of *Ruh* as an infusion from a higher system — a breath or command that enables self-awareness and higher thought. It is not a personal possession, but a shared system-level capacity:

> **"Then He fashioned him and breathed into him from His Ruh..."**
> *(Quran 32:9)*

The word used here is *min Ruhihi* — from *His Ruh*, not a separate or new Ruh. This points to *Ruh* as an emanation of a greater universal consciousness.

Ruh vs. Nafs: Differentiating the Inner Systems

One of the core confusions in religious tradition is the conflation of *Ruh* with *Nafs* (self or ego). The Quran treats these as two distinct entities:

- **Nafs** represents the personal, emotional, and reactive self — the psychological being influenced by desires, fears, and memories.
- **Ruh** represents the system of consciousness that enables self-awareness, morality, and understanding — a neutral, non-emotional interface with higher purpose.

In scientific terms, *Ruh* could be understood as the neurological potential for conscious reflection — while *Nafs* is the product of environmental, social, and psychological inputs processed through memory and emotion.

Breath of Life or Switch of Awareness?

The Quranic metaphor of God "breathing" into Adam is not a physical act. It represents the point where the human form acquired the capacity for higher cognition. In embryology, there is a stage when the brain's neocortex begins to function — allowing for memory, language acquisition, and complex perception.

The timing of *Ruh* being "breathed" into the fetus aligns metaphorically with this stage. The Quran does not mention *Ruh* being inserted at fertilization, but after human formation:

"...then We made him into another creation..." *(Quran 23:14)*

This "another creation" points toward the emergence of awareness — the conscious human being. This view resonates with how *Ruh* represents not life itself, but a transformation of the *type* of life: from biological to conscious.

Quantum Consciousness and the System of Amr

Recent quantum theories (e.g., Penrose-Hameroff's Orch-OR model) suggest that consciousness may be rooted in quantum processes in microtubules within neurons. These processes may interact with universal fields of information.

This provides a scientific counterpart to the Quranic concept of *amr* — the systemic, command-level process through which *Ruh* operates. In other words, *Ruh* may be the capacity within the brain to align with universal informational flows — making human beings capable of insight, ethics, and awareness beyond instinct.

Misuse of Ruh in Religious Culture

Over centuries, religious scholars have transformed *Ruh* into an immortal, floating soul — complete with descriptions of its exit during death and travel to heavens. These views have no Quranic basis.

The Quran never says that *Ruh* is independent, nor that it survives as an individual entity. Instead, the Quran repeatedly describes death as the *completion* of one's life circuit:

"Every Nafs shall taste death..." *(Quran 3:185)*

The emphasis is on the *Nafs* (self), not *Ruh*, tasting death. This suggests *Ruh* is not a separate being but a functionality that ceases when the body ceases to sustain it — like electricity going out when a bulb breaks.

Ruh and Ethical Intelligence

According to Quran, *Ruh* enables *hearing, seeing, and feeling* — but not just in a sensory way. It enhances moral perception:

> **"And made for you hearing, sight, and hearts — little do you give thanks."** *(Quran 32:9)*

Here, *Qulub* (interpreted as hearts, but actually referring to mental centers) are linked with the infusion of *Ruh*. This implies that *Ruh* activates ethical intelligence — our ability to reflect, empathize, and choose right from wrong. It is the driver of what we call moral cognition.

Conclusion: Reclaiming Ruh

To reclaim *Ruh* from centuries of mysticism, we must view it through the dual lens of the Quran's system-based language and today's emerging scientific understanding of consciousness. *Ruh* is not a ghost but a program — a divine operating system embedded within the biological hardware of the human brain.

It connects humans to a higher moral logic, enables awareness of self and others, and allows us to rise above mere survival toward meaningful existence.

In essence, *Ruh* is the divine spark of universal consciousness that makes us truly human.

Chapter 6: The Forbidden Tree — What Did Adam Really Eat?

The story of Adam eating from the "forbidden tree" is one of the most pivotal yet misunderstood narratives within the Abrahamic traditions. In popular interpretations, this act is reduced to a mere disobedience involving a fruit — often symbolized as an apple. However, when examined through the lens of Quranic linguistics, cognitive science, and human psychology, the narrative transforms into a profound insight into the emergence of moral consciousness and free will.

This chapter deconstructs the symbolic nature of the "tree," the concept of prohibition, and the psychological implications of the act of "eating" in the Quranic framework. Rather than a literal event, the Quran presents this story as a layered allegory that explains humanity's transition into a being with cognitive awareness, moral agency, and the burden of ethical choice.

The Quranic Narrative — Tree as Allegory

Quranic Verses:

> "But Satan whispered to him. He said: 'O Adam! Shall I lead you to the Tree of Eternity and a kingdom that never decays?'" (Surah Taha 20:120)

> "But do not go near this tree, lest you become wrongdoers." (Surah Al-Baqarah 2:35)

The Quran does not mention the name of the tree, nor does it describe it as a fruit-bearing botanical species. Instead, it emphasizes the *action* of nearing and partaking from it. The Arabic term used for tree is **"Shajarah"**, which is also etymologically connected with **"tashajur"** — meaning conflict, contradiction, or branching disputes. This suggests that the tree is symbolic of complex moral choices and cognitive branching that leads to ethical dilemmas.

In this light, the forbidden tree becomes a metaphor for moral reasoning — a branching decision-making process involving right and wrong, consequences and responsibility.

The Psychology of Temptation and Awareness

Satan's temptation is not about hunger or physical need. Instead, it appeals to:

- **Eternity (Khold)**
- **Power (Mulk la yabla)**

These are desires deeply embedded in the human psyche — the longing for immortality and control. The moment Adam responds to these desires marks the **birth of psychological ego** and **moral conflict.**

In neuropsychology, this aligns with the awakening of the **prefrontal cortex** — the part of the brain responsible for abstract thought, foresight, moral judgment, and decision-making.

> **Hypothesis:** The act of eating from the tree symbolizes the *activation* of cognitive consciousness — the ability to reflect, make choices, and recognize consequences. It's the origin point of ethical selfhood.

The Act of Eating — Not Just Digestion

In Quranic usage, the act of eating (**Akal**) often represents **internalizing knowledge or behavior.** For example:

> "Those who consume interest will not stand [on the Day of Resurrection] except as one stands who is being beaten by Satan into insanity." (Surah Al-Baqarah 2:275)

Here, eating is equated with adopting a lifestyle based on exploitation. Similarly, in the Adam narrative, "eating from the tree" can be interpreted as the internalization of the knowledge of duality — good vs evil, right vs wrong.

Thus, the story becomes a **psychological blueprint** for the birth of ethical cognition.

Was It a Sin or a Necessary Step?

The Quran's tone regarding Adam's act is not one of wrath, but of guidance:

> "Then his Lord chose him and turned to him in forgiveness and guided him." (Surah Taha 20:122)

This implies that the event was not a fall, but a **transition.** It marked the beginning of human responsibility — **Takleef** — the moment where humans became morally accountable beings.

> "We have indeed created man in hardship." (Surah Al-Balad 90:4)

The hardship here is not punishment, but the burden of choice and consequence that comes with consciousness.

Scientific Parallels — The Cognitive Leap

The emergence of moral reasoning in human evolution is tied to the development of **theory of mind** — the ability to recognize that others have thoughts and intentions. This is a major cognitive leap unique to homo sapiens.

Experiments show that only humans (and to some extent, certain primates) can:

- Anticipate the consequences of actions
- Experience guilt or regret
- Plan long-term

This aligns perfectly with the Quranic depiction of Adam as the first being to bear the burden of moral choice.

Free Will — The Gift and the Test

The essence of the Adam story is the **gift of free will** — not just the ability to choose, but to choose **rightly.**

> "Indeed, We guided him to the way, be he grateful or ungrateful."
> (Surah Al-Insan 76:3)

The forbidden tree is not about divine restriction, but about **moral awareness.** The command was a boundary to test awareness — not an arbitrary law.

Summary — What Did Adam Really Eat?

Adam did not eat a fruit. He *internalized* consciousness, decision-making, and moral responsibility. The tree was symbolic of:

- **The branching logic of free will**
- **Temptation toward power and permanence**
- **The awakening of ethical selfhood**

The eating was not a fall from grace but a step into maturity — from **biological existence** to **moral agency.**

Conclusion: The Forbidden Tree as the First Ethical Choice

Through a synthesis of Quranic symbolism, cognitive psychology, and evolutionary biology, the story of the forbidden tree reveals the core of what makes us human — not just life, but **conscious life** capable of reflection, guilt, and responsibility.

The narrative shifts from being a tale of sin to being a **blueprint of conscious evolution.** It wasn't a mistake, it was a transformation — the humanization of Homo sapiens.

Chapter 7: The Descent from Paradise — Metaphor of Moral Responsibility

The concept of Adam's "descent from Paradise" has often been portrayed as an expulsion due to sin — a fall from divine favor. But when we reexamine this narrative through the lens of Quranic linguistics, symbolic analysis, and modern cognitive development, it reveals a much deeper reality: the moment Adam was entrusted with moral agency, he transitioned from a state of innocence (paradise) into a world governed by responsibility, cause-effect, and consequence.

This chapter argues that Paradise (*Jannah*) in the Quranic context is not a geographical or botanical space, but a symbolic description of a pre-responsible psychological state — akin to early human cognition before the awakening of ethical reasoning. The "descent" represents the human transition into accountability, awareness, and societal function.

Quranic Verses and Linguistic Analysis

> "We said: Go down from it, all of you. And when guidance comes to you from Me, whoever follows My guidance will not fear nor grieve." (Surah Al-Baqarah 2:38)

> "Then his Lord chose him and turned to him in forgiveness and guided him." (Surah Taha 20:122)

The Arabic word **"ihbitu"** (اهبطوا) translated as "descend" or "go down" comes from the root *"habata"*, which is also used in the Quran to describe the transition from one state to another — not necessarily geographically, but functionally and spiritually:

> "And We said: Strike the rock with your staff. Then twelve springs gushed from it... and do not act wickedly on earth, spreading corruption. And when you said: O Moses! We will not endure one kind of food... so send for us from the produce of the earth... He said:

> Would you exchange that which is better for that which is worse? Go down (*ihbitu*) to any town, and you will find what you have asked for." (Surah Al-Baqarah 2:60-61)

Clearly, *ihbitu* refers to a **change in condition or mode of life** — from ease to responsibility, from instinct to decision-making.

Paradise as a Psychological State

In classical interpretations, Jannah is portrayed as a literal garden. However, the Quran never describes this specific Jannah as the ultimate paradise of the afterlife. Rather, it represents a state of comfort, security, and innocence.

From a cognitive and developmental psychology viewpoint, this aligns with the **pre-moral stage of human cognition** — a time when humans (and human societies) operated primarily on instinct and had no concept of moral consequences.

Adam's stay in Jannah represents the **prenatal or pre-conscious phase** — a period of existence without ethical burden.

The Fall as a Rise in Moral Burden

The descent did not occur because Adam sinned, but because Adam reached the cognitive level at which he became **capable of responsibility.**

> "Then We said: Go down, some of you as enemies to others, and on earth will be a dwelling place and provision for a time." (Surah Al-A'raf 7:24)

The hostility mentioned — *"some of you as enemies to others"* — reflects the **emergence of social competition, tribalism, ego, and conflict** — characteristics of complex societies. These are only possible when moral self-awareness is present.

Hence, the descent marks the birth of **civilization and society** — a world where human actions have ripple effects on others.

From Shelter to Struggle — The Symbol of Earth

> "On earth will be your dwelling place and your livelihood for a time."
> (Surah Al-A'raf 7:24)

The Earth here symbolizes a domain of causality, effort, and labor — *the realm of takleef* (responsibility).

In embryological parallels, this matches the **postnatal transition** — from the comfort of the womb to the effort-based world of survival and self-sufficiency. Similarly, in evolutionary history, it represents the stage when Homo sapiens began to:

- Organize into societies
- Create tools
- Develop laws and moral codes

Thus, Earth in this verse is not punishment — it is **the arena of ethical choice and development.**

Forgiveness Before Accountability

An essential part of the story is the divine forgiveness that occurs **before** the descent:

> "Then Adam received words from his Lord, and He turned to him in mercy. Indeed, He is the Accepting of repentance, the Merciful."
> (Surah Al-Baqarah 2:37)

This suggests that the descent was not a result of condemnation, but a **planned phase of growth** — the next step in conscious evolution. In developmental terms, it is like a child learning to walk and falling; the fall is not punished but understood as part of learning.

Symbolism of Clothing and Shame

> "So he caused them to fall by deception. And when they tasted of the tree, their private parts became apparent to them, and they began to cover themselves with the leaves of Paradise." (Surah Al-A'raf 7:22)

This verse aligns with the emergence of **social self-consciousness and shame** — uniquely human traits. Only humans wear clothes and are aware of nudity in a moral sense. This reflects the birth of:

- **Social awareness**
- **Ego**
- **Moral emotions like guilt and embarrassment**

From a neurological standpoint, these behaviors are regulated by the **limbic system and prefrontal cortex** — which mature as the brain evolves and develops in both species and individuals.

Conclusion — Descent as Emergence

The descent of Adam from Paradise is not a literal fall to Earth or a punishment, but a **metaphorical rise into consciousness.**

It marks:

- The transition from instinct to moral responsibility
- The beginning of social structure and ethical choice
- The shift from passive existence to active accountability

This reinterpretation removes the guilt-ridden lens imposed by later theological interpretations and reframes the story as a **celebration of human maturity.**

> Adam did not fall — he rose into responsibility.
>
> Paradise was not lost — it was transformed into moral potential.

Chapter 8: Iblis – The Psychological Ego and Rebellion Against Reason

The figure of Iblis in the Quran is often imagined as a supernatural being—sometimes equated with a fire-based creature or a fallen angel. Traditional interpretations, heavily influenced by myth and mysticism, have clouded the Quranic portrayal of Iblis. In this chapter, we will deconstruct the character of Iblis not as a mythical jinni but as a deep psychological archetype that reflects the human ego, arrogance, and rebellion against rational guidance.

Iblis in Quranic Language: Beyond the Myth

The word *Iblis* comes from the root "balasa," which means to despair or become hopeless. Iblis is not described in the Quran as a fallen angel but as one "from among the jinn" (Surah Al-Kahf, 18:50). However, this term 'jinn' does not imply a literal fire-being but instead refers to hidden or unseen entities—potentially thoughts, emotions, or forces within the psyche that are not physically visible.

Iblis is presented as a being who had access to divine knowledge, who worshipped among angels, and who possessed the ability to choose. When commanded to bow before Adam—a symbol of higher consciousness and collective human evolution—Iblis refused.

> "He said, 'I am better than him: You created me from fire, and You created him from clay.'" (Surah Al-A'raf, 7:12)

This refusal is not based on logic but on arrogance, pride, and comparison—hallmarks of an inflated ego. The 'fire' represents impulsive energy, dominance, and pride, while 'clay' symbolizes groundedness, potential, and humility. Iblis chooses pride over submission to a rational, ethical order.

Psychological Profile of Iblis: Ego in Revolt

Iblis can be seen as a metaphor for the human *nafs al-ammarah*—the commanding self that resists moral discipline and rational thought. His behavior reveals traits such as:

1. **Narcissism** – A belief in one's superiority, refusal to acknowledge the progress of others.
2. **Deflection of Responsibility** – He blames Allah for his misguidance: *"Because You have led me astray..."* (Surah Al-Hijr, 15:39)
3. **Isolationism** – He withdraws from a community that follows divine logic and wants to mislead others to justify his own failure.
4. **Obsessive Rebellion** – He is not interested in growth but in defiance for its own sake.

In psychology, these align with the traits of sociopathic behavior and antisocial personality disorder—where reason is subordinated to selfish impulse and the denial of accountability.

The Refusal to Bow: A Symbol of Intellectual Stagnation

The command to bow to Adam symbolizes submission to the evolved moral and rational framework that humanity is meant to follow. Iblis' refusal is symbolic of the mind that refuses to submit to higher reasoning, ethical responsibility, and universal truth.

His logic, *"I am better than him"*, is the same logic behind racism, casteism, sexism, and supremacy ideologies. It reflects a deep-rooted psychological illusion that one's origin determines one's worth. This is the rebellion not just against God, but against the natural progression of consciousness toward justice, equality, and rationality.

The Fire Within: What 'Created from Fire' Really Means

When Iblis says he was created from fire, this can be understood metaphorically. Fire represents energy, speed, power—but also destructiveness.

The clay from which Adam is made is the same material that enables life to grow. Clay is adaptive, nurturing, and evolves slowly but purposefully.

Iblis represents the mind that prioritizes instant gratification, emotion over reason, and dominance over cooperation. Fire burns quickly, consumes rapidly, and leaves ashes. Clay builds, nurtures, and sustains.

Iblis and Free Will: An Abuse of Choice

Iblis was given free will. He chose rebellion. But unlike Adam, who repented, Iblis doubled down. He used his free will to justify error instead of correcting it. His punishment is not imposed—it is self-inflicted through his refusal to evolve. The Quranic account shows that Iblis' fall is not due to lack of knowledge but due to moral arrogance and emotional rigidity.

The Mission of Deception: Psychological Projection

Iblis vows to mislead humans:

> "I will sit in wait for them on Your straight path..." (Surah Al-A'raf, 7:16)

This isn't a literal creature whispering from behind trees. It reflects the psychological battle within us. The ego (Iblis) resists any form of accountability, resents submission to truth, and constantly rationalizes wrongdoing. He sits on the 'straight path' because even people on a righteous path are vulnerable to self-deception and arrogance.

Conclusion: The Real Enemy Within

Iblis is not an external monster; he is the internal voice that whispers rebellion against wisdom. He is not a creature made of fire but a psychological construct made of pride, prejudice, and fear. The real *Shaitan* is not one being but a pattern of thought.

Understanding Iblis as a symbol of the ego, irrational pride, and emotional rebellion gives us a clearer, science-compatible and spiritually mature view of the Quranic message. This reading invites us not to fear an invisible devil, but to overcome the inner tendency to deny truth, avoid responsibility, and inflate our own superiority.

The downfall of Iblis was not because he lacked faith—but because he refused reason. His story is a reminder that arrogance, when left unchecked, leads to moral and intellectual collapse.

This is not a tale of mythical beings. It is the psychological anatomy of every human soul standing between rational evolution and egotistic stagnation.

Chapter 9: The First Human Society — Adam as the Social Prototype

The story of Adam is not merely about the emergence of a biological individual; it is the story of a transformation — the birth of social consciousness. To understand Adam solely as a physical being is to miss the Quran's multidimensional narrative that uses Adam as a metaphor for the rise of human intelligence, ethics, and organized society. In this chapter, we explore how Adam represents the foundation of social structures, the evolution of cooperation, and the birth of moral responsibility.

Adam as "Khalifa": A Social Appointment, not a Religious Title

In Surah Al-Baqarah (2:30), the Quran says:

> "Indeed, I will place upon the earth a *Khalifa*."

This word *Khalifa* has often been translated as "vicegerent" or "deputy of God," leading to mystical or political interpretations. However, the root of the word "Khalafa" means "to come after," "to succeed," or "to leave behind." The term *Khalifa* in this context points toward succession and continuity — not divine monarchy.

This appointment is made **on Earth** (fil-ard), not in the heavens. It is a designation of *worldly responsibility*, not spiritual royalty. The term *Khalifa* thus indicates the emergence of a being capable of maintaining order, cooperating with others, and forming a society guided by reason, not just instinct.

In simple terms: **Adam is not a religious leader. Adam is a cognitive leap. A conscious being capable of societal order and collective responsibility.**

From Solitary Intelligence to Cooperative Consciousness

Prior to Adam, creatures lived in hierarchical, instinct-driven societies. What Adam symbolizes is the shift from instinctive survival to **moral choice**,

dialogue, **conflict resolution**, and **cooperative intelligence**. This evolution marks the formation of human society.

Adam becomes the prototype of this shift:

- He is taught "names" (Surah Al-Baqarah 2:31), which symbolize classification, language, abstraction.
- He recognizes his mistake and accepts correction — a unique moral trait.
- He receives *guidance* (huda) and is told to follow it with others, indicating the beginning of social learning and structured laws.

These are not traits of an individual animal, but of a species stepping into organized communal life.

Human Society: From Tool Use to Moral Governance

What separates Adam from other creatures is not the physical structure, but **the internal law — the conscience**. The moment humans began organizing, negotiating, planning, and creating moral codes, the Adamic phase began.

This social emergence can be understood in stages:

1. **Basic Grouping** – Early humans gathered in small tribes.
2. **Cooperation and Sharing** – Language and memory allowed knowledge to be shared, not just instinctively passed.
3. **Conflict Resolution** – With intellect and morality, humans developed rules.
4. **Justice and Ethics** – The concepts of fairness, accountability, and communal welfare emerged.

Adam is the symbol of this **moral awakening**, not merely of the biological birth.

Moral Responsibility: The Key to Being Human

The Quran constantly links Adam's narrative with **responsibility and accountability**. Adam is not punished for curiosity, but for **disobedience and lack of discipline**. Yet, unlike Iblis, Adam accepts fault and **seeks correction**:

> "They said, 'Our Lord, we have wronged ourselves...'" (Surah Al-A'raf 7:23)

This act of self-reflection is the cornerstone of ethical society. The Adamic model includes:

- **Acknowledgment of error**
- **Seeking reform**
- **Learning through experience**
- **Choosing communal order over individual pride**

These are foundational traits of any progressive society.

The Human Being as a Social Mirror

The Quran does not mention Adam living alone. The social dimension is implied throughout:

- He is taught to communicate.
- He is warned of ego (Iblis).
- He is instructed to follow divine guidance **with others.**
- He is part of a fall and rise that includes shared consequences.

This mirrors real-world human development. Our survival has never been based on isolation but on **family, tribe, city, and civilization**.

Adam, in this light, is the first social being — the prototype of the modern human mind and communal behavior.

Beyond Gender and Family Myths

The Quranic narrative of Adam is not gender-focused. The name "Hawwa" is not even mentioned in the Quran. Nor is there any justification for patriarchal dominance. Instead, what emerges is a shared human responsibility.

The descent of Adam is not a fall from grace, but a **transition from innocence to responsibility** — from pre-societal instincts to organized moral life.

Conclusion: Adam as a Living Blueprint of Society

Adam is not a myth, nor is he a magical figure. Adam is **us** — the social species capable of creating peace or chaos. The *Khalifa* status is not a crown but a contract: a call to build, to think, to lead with reason and justice.

Understanding Adam as the social prototype reframes the Quranic message from a story of origin to a manual for civilizational growth. It invites humanity not to worship the past, but to evolve the present.

Chapter 10: Language, Memory, and the Naming Power — The Cognitive Shift in Adam

One of the most intellectually profound and symbolically rich verses in the Quran is the following:

> *"And He taught Adam the names — all of them. Then He presented them to the angels and said, 'Inform Me of the names of these, if you are truthful.'"*
>
> *(Surah Al-Baqarah 2:31)*

This brief verse opens the door to one of humanity's greatest evolutionary milestones — **language**. But it also speaks of more than speech. Embedded in this Quranic verse is the seed of **naming, classification, memory, identity, knowledge, and consciousness**. To "know the names" is to have access to cognitive tools that made humans not only intelligent but self-aware, collaborative, and morally accountable.

This chapter explores the scientific and psychological dimensions of this "naming power," and how it relates to Adam — not as one man, but as a symbolic prototype of cognitive humanity.

What Does "Teaching the Names" Really Mean?

Let us first examine the linguistic significance.

The Arabic phrase used is *"wa 'allama Adama al-asma'a kullaha"* — "He taught Adam all the names." The word *asma'* (أسماء) is the plural of *ism* (اسم), which means *name*, but also signifies *identity*, *distinction*, *designation*, and *categorization*.

Names are not just sounds. In linguistic science, **a name is a symbol assigned to a concept**. Naming something involves:

- Identifying a distinct pattern or object in reality
- Abstracting its features
- Creating a symbol (word) to represent it
- Memorizing and transmitting that symbol to others

In this light, the Quranic verse is not just talking about verbal vocabulary. It's about the **cognitive ability to abstract reality, assign meaning, and transmit ideas.** This is the root of human civilization.

Language: The Defining Leap in Human Evolution

From a scientific perspective, the emergence of symbolic language marks the *true evolutionary break* between humans and other hominids.

While other animals communicate, none possess:

- **Grammar**: The structuring of thoughts through rules
- **Displacement**: The ability to speak of things not present
- **Symbolism**: The use of words to represent abstract ideas
- **Recursive thought**: Thoughts about thoughts, imagination

This evolution of language is directly tied to the **development of the neocortex** and particularly **Broca's and Wernicke's areas** in the brain, which govern language production and comprehension.

The Quranic concept of "teaching names" mirrors exactly this evolutionary leap — where thought is no longer bound to the immediate environment, but extends to the symbolic, conceptual, and even spiritual domains.

Memory and Internal Representation

To name something, one must **first remember and recall it**. Naming is useless without memory. The Quran's reference to Adam's unique ability to retain and communicate names implies the emergence of long-term memory and **internal mapping of the external world**.

Memory serves several functions in this framework:

- **Storage of learned information**
- **Retrieval for communication**
- **Anticipation of future outcomes based on past knowledge**
- **Moral judgment, which relies on the memory of consequences**

This ability is entirely absent in angels (as described in the verse), and in all other forms of pre-Adamic creation, according to the Quran.

The angels' reply confirms this:

> *"They said: Glory be to You! We have no knowledge except what You have taught us. Indeed, you are the All-Knowing, the All-Wise."*
>
> *(Surah Al-Baqarah 2:32)*

This admission reveals that Adam's naming power signifies a **new level of consciousness**, surpassing even the intuitive perfection of angels.

The Connection Between Naming and Responsibility

Naming is not a neutral act. In psychology and philosophy, **to name something is to define it, categorize it, and take responsibility for how it is understood**.

For instance:

- Naming an emotion allows us to manage it.
- Naming an illness allows us to treat it.
- Naming injustice allows us to correct it.

Adam's ability to name is the beginning of **moral agency**. This cognitive step allows humans to build societies, justice systems, sciences, and philosophies. Without naming, there is only chaos — everything remains undefined, fluid, and confusing.

The Challenge to the Angels: Knowledge Over Obedience

In the Quran, God does not demonstrate Adam's superiority through power or miracles, but through **knowledge**. This is a sharp break from earlier mythologies in which divine beings are defined by force or supernatural traits.

By having Adam name what the angels could not, the Quran makes a bold claim:

Humanity's value lies not in submission, but in understanding.

This knowledge is not inherited, but taught: *"He taught Adam..."* — meaning knowledge is a process, a developmental journey, not a divine gift. Adam, and therefore mankind, is not infallible but educable. That is the true honor of humanity.

Naming, Identity, and Modern Cognition

In modern neuroscience and cognitive linguistics, naming and categorization are considered key stages of consciousness:

1. **Sensory Input** – We observe the world through senses.
2. **Cognitive Encoding** – The brain processes what is seen/heard/felt.
3. **Labeling** – The brain assigns names or meanings.
4. **Storage in Memory** – The brain stores it for recall.
5. **Retrieval and Expression** – The brain communicates it through speech or symbols.

Adam's story, viewed through this lens, is a **neuroscientific prophecy** — describing how a creature became self-aware and socially intelligent.

Beyond Literalism: Adam as Every Human Child

Interestingly, every human child replicates the Adamic process in early development:

- Babies begin with sensory perception.
- Then they mimic sounds.

- Gradually, they assign names to objects.
- Later, they understand categories (animal, object, feeling).
- Finally, they use language abstractly and socially.

This means every child undergoes a **miniature re-creation of Adam** — transitioning from instinct to intelligence. The "teaching of names" is not a one-time event, but a universal human process encoded in our biology.

Conclusion: Naming as the Dawn of Humanity

In the Quranic framework, Adam becomes Adam not when he is formed from clay, but when he begins to **name, remember, and transmit**. That is the moment the dust becomes divine — when consciousness emerges, and thought meets expression.

This chapter is not about the origin of words, but about the **origin of consciousness**, of shared meaning, and of collective identity. It is about the turning point in evolution when a species stepped beyond survival and into civilization.

In the next chapter, we will explore how the Quranic terms *Qalb*, *Sadr*, and *Fu'ad* represent specific layers of human cognition and emotional decision-making — bringing us closer to understanding how our brain reflects the inner universe revealed in the Quran.

Chapter 11: Qalb, Sadr, and Fu'ad — The Inner System of Human Decisions

(From the Quranic, Psychological, and Neuroscientific Perspective)

The Quran does not use simplistic terms to describe the human mind or soul. Instead, it presents a multilayered structure of human cognition, emotion, and decision-making using precise Arabic terms such as **Qalb** (**قلب**), **Sadr** (**صدر**), and **Fu'ad** (**فؤاد**). These terms are often mistranslated or misunderstood, with "Qalb" commonly translated as "heart," "Sadr" as "chest," and "Fu'ad" again as a kind of emotional heart.

However, when we move away from literal anatomy and explore these words through the lens of cognitive science, psychology, and Quranic context, a far more intricate and scientifically accurate picture emerges — a model of the **human inner system of perception, emotional processing, and judgment**.

Qalb (قلب): The Center of Cognitive Consciousness

Quranic Use:

The term "Qalb" appears over 130 times in the Quran. It is described as:

- Capable of reasoning (*ta'aqqul*)
- Capable of perception (*tafakkur*)
- Capable of understanding and turning away
- Susceptible to being "locked" or "diseased"
- The seat of faith or hypocrisy

"They have hearts (Qulub) with which they do not understand..."

(Surah Al-A'raf 7:179)

> *"In their Qulub is a disease, so Allah has increased their disease."*
>
> *(Surah Al-Baqarah 2:10)*

Scientific Interpretation:

Contrary to the common assumption that the "heart" is purely an emotional center, the **Quran describes Qalb as the place where reasoning, awareness, and moral judgment occur**. In modern terms, this aligns not with the physical heart, but with the **prefrontal cortex and associated neural networks** involved in:

- **Abstract thinking**
- **Moral reasoning**
- **Self-regulation**
- **Critical analysis**

Thus, Qalb in the Quran represents **cognitive consciousness** — the **decision-making and reflective self**, not the seat of emotion alone.

Conclusion:

Qalb is best understood as the **higher-order cognitive processor** — the faculty that evaluates, questions, believes, disbelieves, repents, or resists. It is the **moral intellect**.

Sadr (صدر): The Subconscious or Emotional Surface

Quranic Use:

"Sadr" literally means "chest" or "upper torso," but in the Quran it is used metaphorically to refer to:

- The place where **Satan whispers**
- The region where **feelings of anxiety, pride, arrogance, or doubt** take root
- The place where **guidance or tightness** resides

"Who whispers in the chests (sudur) of mankind."

(Surah An-Naas 114:5)

"So that He may make what Satan casts a trial for those in whose chests is a disease."

(Surah Al-Hajj 22:53)

"And We remove whatever is in their chests of resentment..."

(Surah Al-A'raf 7:43)

Scientific Interpretation:

"Sadr" represents the **emotional interface** between the external world and inner processing. In neuroscience, this is similar to the **limbic system**, which processes:

- **Emotional reactions**
- **Fear, anxiety, and pleasure**
- **Fight-or-flight responses**
- **Social memory**

Sadr is where **emotions arise**, but before they are fully processed or evaluated by Qalb.

Conclusion:

Sadr represents the **emotional surface** or **subconscious interface** — where raw feelings, instincts, and whisperings (internal or external) first appear.

Fu'ad (فُؤَاد): The Flame of Intense Emotion and Focus

Quranic Use:

Fu'ad is often used in the Quran in emotionally charged contexts — representing **passionate, burning emotion**, a more volatile and intense inner state than Qalb or Sadr.

"The Fu'ad of the mother of Musa became empty."

(Surah Al-Qasas 28:10)

"The hearing, the vision, and the Fu'ad — each will be questioned."

(Surah Al-Isra 17:36)

Fu'ad is not used lightly; it is invoked when emotion overwhelms or drives action.

Scientific Interpretation:

Fu'ad can be likened to **acute affective focus** — moments when the **amygdala, hypothalamus**, and **emotional centers of the brain** override rational thought, pushing action based on intense emotional surge. It is the **burning center of love, fear, grief, or desire**.

Conclusion:

Fu'ad represents the **emotional core**, activated in moments of crisis, passion, or obsession. It is **not always rational**, but intensely human.

Integrative Model: The Inner Map of the Human Experience

From the Quranic structure, we can map the human internal process as follows:

1. **Sadr** receives raw input — instincts, whisperings, fears, desires. It is emotionally sensitive, easily disturbed.
2. **Fu'ad** amplifies and ignites certain feelings — causing burning urgency or paralysis.
3. **Qalb** reflects on these impulses, balances them with values, wisdom, and deeper awareness, and **decides**.

Each of these faculties is also vulnerable:

- Sadr can be **tightened or expanded**.
- Fu'ad can be **overwhelmed**.
- Qalb can become **hardened, diseased, or locked**.

The Quran acknowledges this vulnerability, which is why it calls for **Tazkiyah** (purification), **Tawbah** (turning), and **Zikr** (remembrance) — practices that realign and cleanse these layers.

Why the Quran Uses Multiple Terms Instead of One

Western thought often simplifies the mind into "heart vs. brain" or "emotion vs. reason." But the Quran presents a **multilayered consciousness**, acknowledging that humans are:

- **Instinctual (Sadr)**
- **Emotional (Fu'ad)**
- **Rational and moral (Qalb)**

This model reflects a deep, pre-modern awareness of **human psychological complexity** — now confirmed by neuroscience.

Final Insight: How These Terms Guide Personal Development

Each term corresponds not just to a part of the brain or emotional life, but to **a stage of human evolution and maturity**:

- A child starts with **Sadr** — reacting to the world emotionally.
- With age, intense **Fu'ad** moments' drive learning and identity formation.
- With reflection, **Qalb** is activated — and humans become morally accountable beings.

The Quran, in guiding humans to use their Qalb, is not preaching to the emotions alone — it is calling us to the **higher cognitive self**, rooted in reason, morality, and humility.

Chapter 12: The Mirror Test — When Did Human Beings Become Self-Aware?

From Reflection to Realization: Tracing the Rise of Conscious Identity in Homo Sapiens

What makes us human? It is not just our upright posture, tool-making ability, or complex language—it is our **self-awareness**. The Quran hints at the evolution of this cognitive leap by describing Adam being taught names (Surah Al-Baqarah 2:31), the refusal of Iblis to bow, and Adam's descent into responsibility. Science, on the other hand, explores this threshold through **neurological development** and **the mirror test**—a symbolic and experimental marker of self-recognition. This chapter connects the Quranic narrative of Adam's awakening with scientific experiments, exploring when and how human beings first became **self-aware individuals.**

What is Self-Awareness?

Self-awareness is not simply being alive or reacting to stimuli. It is the capacity to recognize oneself as a distinct entity, possessing a mind, emotions, and thoughts. This includes:

- **Mirror self-recognition**
- **Empathy and theory of mind**
- **Self-control and ethical choice**
- **Abstract thinking and internal narrative**

This is what elevated Adam, not physically, but cognitively and ethically, into a **new category of being.**

The Mirror Test: A Scientific Tool

The **mirror test** was developed by psychologist **Gordon Gallup Jr.** in the 1970s. It involves placing a visible mark on an animal's face and then exposing it to a mirror. If the animal touches or investigates the mark on its own body (not the reflection), it demonstrates **self-recognition.**

Species that have passed this test include:

- Humans (typically from 18 to 24 months of age)
- Great apes (chimpanzees, bonobos, orangutans)
- Dolphins
- Elephants
- Magpies

Among these, **only humans develop extended self-narratives**, complex language, and abstract moral reasoning.

Quranic Insight: Teaching of Names and the Emergence of Self

Surah Al-Baqarah 2:31 says:

> "And He taught Adam the names—all of them. Then He showed them to the angels..."

This passage is often taken to refer to linguistic ability, but deeper reflection shows it **symbolizes the emergence of identity**, categorization, memory, and abstraction—**core components of consciousness.** The act of naming is not just vocabulary—it is classification, projection, intention, and awareness of distinction. Naming includes not just external objects but also inner states: *I am sad, I desire, I regret.*

This is the **dawn of self-awareness**, and it marks the difference between pre-human creatures and **Homo sapiens**, the fully conscious being.

The Age of Consciousness: Archaeological Evidence

Human fossils date back millions of years, but self-awareness likely emerged much later. Let's examine **archaeological indicators** of cognitive modernity:

- **Burial rituals (100,000–120,000 years ago)**: Indicates understanding of death and abstract identity.
- **Cave paintings (40,000–60,000 years ago)**: Suggest imaginative projection and memory.
- **Ornamental use of shells and pigments (70,000–90,000 years ago)**: Symbolic behavior, possibly reflecting self-image.
- **Tool complexity**: Planning, refinement, and future projection.

These are not just artifacts; they are **material evidence of an internal mirror**—a growing ability to see oneself as "I."

The Link Between the Brain and Self-Recognition

Modern neuroscience has identified certain areas in the human brain that are involved in **self-awareness**:

- **Prefrontal cortex**: Critical for decision-making and moral reasoning.
- **Temporo-parietal junction**: Involved in distinguishing between self and others.
- **Default mode network**: Activates when a person is engaged in inward-focused tasks like daydreaming, memory recall, and self-reflection.

This network is **hyperactive in humans** compared to all other known species, suggesting a neurological basis for the Quranic idea of Adam's awakening—his recognition of responsibility, guilt, and purpose.

The Mirror in the Mind: A Quranic Reinterpretation

When Adam becomes aware of his mistake, he seeks forgiveness (Surah Al-A'raf 7:23):

> "Our Lord, we have wronged ourselves..."

This is not primitive behavior. This is the **birth of conscience**. The acknowledgment of error and moral introspection is the **true test of**

self-awareness. The "mirror" in the Quran is not glass—it is **moral consciousness.**

Mirror Test vs Moral Test

Science gives us a mirror test of physical recognition.

The Quran gives us a **moral mirror test**:

- Can you judge yourself?
- Can you admit error?
- Can you evolve internally?

The first humans to develop this ability **crossed a threshold**—they became "Adam," not by blood, but by awakening.

Conclusion: From Reflection to Responsibility

The journey from **biological evolution** to **moral evolution** marks the real beginning of humanity. The mirror test of science and the **naming test** of the Quran both point toward a common reality: **the rise of self-aware, responsible, ethical beings.**

Adam is not just a man; he is a symbol of the **first conscious mind**, the **moral species**, the **self-reflective Homo sapiens.**

This chapter affirms that the Quran and science are not at war—they are two lights revealing the same truth from different angles.

Chapter 13: The Collective Adam — Genetic and Social Ancestry of Mankind

Unraveling the Biological and Symbolic Origin of Humanity Through Quran and Science

Introduction: Is Adam an Individual or a Collective Symbol?

Traditional interpretations of Adam describe him as the first individual human being created miraculously and uniquely. But deeper linguistic, biological, and philosophical inquiry suggests that "Adam" in the Quran may not refer exclusively to a single person, but to the **collective emergence of human consciousness and responsibility**—a phase in the evolution of Homo sapiens.

This chapter will explore how **genetics**, **evolutionary biology**, and **Quranic language** all converge to support the idea that Adam is both a **symbolic figure and a representation of collective human emergence**, not the originator of the human race in a biological sense.

Quranic Language: Adam as a Prototype, Not Just a Person

The Quran refers to Adam in many places, but never gives biographical details of his physical traits, age, burial, or offspring in the concrete terms typically associated with historical individuals. Instead, we see:

- Adam being taught names (Surah Al-Baqarah 2:31)
- Adam refusing divine limits (Surah Al-A'raf 7:20–22)
- Adam becoming regretful and learning morality
- Adam designated as **Khalifah** (vicegerent), a social function, not just an individual identity

This suggests that Adam is not merely a person, but a **symbolic model of humanity's cognitive and moral awakening**, representing a **collective consciousness**, not merely a single ancestor.

The Genetic Puzzle: No Single Human Ancestor

Biological science has dismantled the myth of a single pair of humans (Adam and Eve) being the origin of all modern humans. Instead:

- **Mitochondrial Eve**: The most recent common matrilineal ancestor of all living humans, likely lived ~150,000–200,000 years ago in Africa.
- **Y-chromosomal Adam**: The most recent patrilineal ancestor, likely lived around 200,000–300,000 years ago—but not at the same time or place as Mitochondrial Eve.
- **Population bottlenecks**: Genetic evidence shows that early humans existed in **groups**, not as a single couple.
- **Interbreeding with Neanderthals and Denisovans**: DNA evidence shows humans interbred with other hominin species.

This strongly implies that the human species emerged **gradually**, and that "Adam" must be understood as a **symbol of a phase** in evolution, not a lone man.

Evolutionary Phases: From Homo to Human

Let's trace the key evolutionary steps toward the emergence of the "Collective Adam":

1. **Australopithecus (4–2 million years ago)**: Walked upright but had limited brain capacity.
2. **Homo habilis (2.4–1.4 million years ago)**: First tool users.
3. **Homo erectus (1.9 million–143,000 years ago)**: Used fire, migrated, had larger brains.
4. **Homo sapiens (300,000 years ago–present)**: Developed art, rituals, language, and eventually **self-awareness**.

The "Adam phase" aligns not with anatomical changes but with the **cognitive leap**—the moment humans began to **name, question, plan, and reflect**. This marks **the birth of the conscious species**, which the Quran symbolically introduces as "Adam."

Social Consciousness: Adam as the Prototype of Civilization

The Quran describes Adam as being given the role of **Khalifah** (Surah Al-Baqarah 2:30):

> "Indeed, I will place upon the Earth a vicegerent (Khalifah)."

This is not a biological description—it is **sociopolitical and moral.** A Khalifah represents the birth of:

- **Ethical systems**
- **Justice and responsibility**
- **Social cooperation and rule-making**
- **Long-term planning and community structures**

These traits are not found in solitary beings but in **social groups** that have developed **self-regulation**, **conscious cooperation**, and **moral codes.** Hence, the "Adam" of the Quran is the **first conscious human society**, not just an individual.

The Role of Memory and Language in Collective Adam

Surah Al-Baqarah 2:31 again becomes central:

> "And He taught Adam the names—all of them..."

Language is not a solo tool; it emerges in **communities.** Naming is impossible without **shared cognition**, **cultural transmission**, and **linguistic evolution.** This supports the scientific view that language and identity evolved **socially**, not through divine instruction to a single person.

Neuroscience also supports this, showing that:

- **Language circuits (Broca's and Wernicke's areas)** evolved gradually

- Mirror neurons enabled **empathy and mimicry**, foundational for communication
- **Cultural evolution** depended on **group interaction**, not isolated beings

The Adam of the Quran therefore represents the **linguistic and social consciousness** of early humans.

Adam and the First Ethical Society

The Quran introduces the first act of **moral awakening** when Adam errs and then repents:

> "Our Lord, we have wronged ourselves..." (Surah Al-A'raf 7:23)

This shows the development of:

- **Moral agency**
- **Guilt and responsibility**
- **Cognitive self-assessment**

These abilities emerge only when **communities evolve rules**, and individuals within them begin to **reflect on their actions**. The Quran is narrating not a fairytale but a **psycho-social evolution**: the first societies becoming ethically aware.

Summary: The Real Adam is All of Us

- Adam is a **collective symbol**, not a single man
- He represents the **first self-aware, socially conscious human communities**
- The Quran's symbolic language harmonizes with **evolutionary biology and genetics**
- Language, responsibility, and ethical codes are **signs of human maturity**, not miracles

The "Collective Adam" is the moment when **biology gave rise to ethics**, and when **genetics was elevated by consciousness**. That is when we became truly human.

Chapter 14: The Journey of Fire and Clay — Evolution of Brain and Body

Decoding Quranic Metaphors Through Science and Neuroscience

Introduction: Clay and Fire — Not Elements, But Metaphors

The Quran repeatedly uses the terms **"Teen"** (**clay**) and **"Naar"** (**fire**) in the creation narrative of humans and jinn. Traditional interpretations view these as literal materials: humans were made of clay, and jinn of smokeless fire. But from a **scientific and linguistic standpoint**, these are not physical ingredients but **metaphoric symbols** for the **evolutionary origin** and **cognitive capacity** of different species.

This chapter will explore how:

- **Clay** represents **biological origin**, grounded in earth-based life and organic chemistry.
- **Fire** represents **neurological energy**, cognition, and higher brain functions like **gamma waves** and **electromagnetic consciousness**.
- Together, these metaphors narrate the **evolution of the human brain-body system**, without contradiction between Quran and science.

Clay: The Organic Chemistry of Life

The Quran uses the word **"Teen"** (clay) and similar terms like:

- **Salsaal** (hard clay)
- **Hama'in masnoon** (dark, fermented mud)
- **Turaab** (dust)

Surah Al-Hijr 15:26:

"And We did certainly create man out of dry clay from an altered black mud."

These terms align with the **clay hypothesis** in origin-of-life science:

1. **Clay as a chemical catalyst**: Clay minerals can trap organic molecules and encourage them to form more complex structures like amino acids and nucleotides—basic building blocks of DNA and proteins.
2. **RNA world and clay surfaces**: Researchers like A.G. Cairns-Smith suggested that **clay particles acted as scaffolding** for RNA replication—essential for the origin of life.
3. **Carbon-based structure**: Life on Earth is based on **carbon, oxygen, hydrogen**, and **nitrogen**—all found abundantly in clay-rich soil.

Thus, "creation from clay" reflects a profound **scientific truth**: our bodies and biological systems evolved from **earth-based organic matter**.

Fire: A Metaphor for Conscious Energy

In contrast, the jinn are described in the Quran as created from **"naar-e-samoom"** (scorching, penetrating fire). Surah Al-Hijr 15:27:

"And the jinn We created earlier from scorching fire."

But what is **fire** in modern physics?

1. **Fire is electromagnetic radiation**: It is **energy**, a process of **rapid oxidation**, not a substance.
2. **Gamma rays and brainwaves**: In neuroscience, **gamma waves** (30–100+ Hz) represent the **highest-frequency brain activity**, linked to:
    - Abstract thought
    - Conscious perception
    - Attention and awareness
    - Binding of memory and sensory experience

3. **The fire of thought**: The **electrical signals and neurotransmitter reactions** in our brain are literally **tiny bursts of electromagnetic energy**.

Thus, **"fire" represents consciousness**, mental energy, and **non-material cognition**, not a physical body. Jinn, in this lens, represent **thought forms, ideas**, or **intelligences** born of fire-like energy.

Human: The Integration of Clay and Fire

The human being is the only creature described in Quran as being:

- Formed from **clay (biological matter)**
- Given **Ruh (spirit/consciousness)**
- Capable of **learning, reflecting, and moral choice**

Surah Sad 38:72:

> "So when I have proportioned him and breathed into him of My Spirit, fall down to him in prostration."

This verse describes the **final synthesis** of the **physical body** and the **cognitive energy**—the transformation from **organic life** to **intelligent being**.

This matches modern neuroscience:

- **Clay (biology)** gives us a **physical brain**, made of lipids, proteins, and water.
- **Fire (neuronal energy)** flows through it as **electric impulses and brainwaves**, giving rise to **consciousness, memory, self-awareness**, and **moral reasoning**.

Hence, the Quran is not contradicting science; it is **compressing thousands of years of evolution** into a **symbolic narrative** accessible to all ages and societies.

The Brain: Fire in Clay

The brain is the **only organ** in the body that is:

- Completely **dependent on electrical impulses**
- Generates **waves of different frequencies** (delta, theta, alpha, beta, gamma)
- Capable of **self-reflection**, abstract logic, and **future planning**

Quranic metaphors like:

- **"Qalb" (mind/heart)**
- **"Sadr" (emotional center)**
- **"Ruh" (spirit/consciousness)**

...all align with **modern models of the brain**, not with the physical heart or chest.

When Allah says He created man from clay and gave him **Ruh**, it is describing the **electrification of biology**, the **illumination of matter by consciousness**—a mystery science is still trying to understand.

Fire and Free Will

"Fire" also symbolizes **free will**, **ego**, and **impulse**. This is demonstrated in the story of Iblis (a jinn):

Surah Al-A'raf 7:12:

> "[Allah] said, 'What prevented you from prostrating when I commanded you?' [Iblis] said, 'I am better than him. You created me from fire and created him from clay.'"

This arrogant claim based on **origin superiority** shows that fire, in excess, leads to:

- **Ego**

- **Pride**
- **Rebellion against order**

It implies that **consciousness without humility**, or **intelligence without responsibility**, becomes dangerous. The Quran presents **Adam as a balanced union**, whereas **Iblis is fire untamed**—a mind that refuses harmony.

Scientific Harmony: Quran and Evolution Are Not Opposed

Let's now combine all these insights:

- **Clay** = Biological evolution, carbon-based life, physical structure
- **Fire** = Consciousness, cognition, brain activity, self-awareness
- **Ruh** = Universal consciousness, purpose, direction of life
- **Adam** = Final product of life + cognition + ethical awareness

The Quranic narrative doesn't reject science—it **summarizes** it symbolically.

Conclusion: You Are Clay That Burns with Thought

You are not just biology, nor just energy. You are a **symphony of elements and intelligence**.

- From the **dust of stars**, your body was formed.
- From the **flame of neural fire**, your thoughts were born.
- From the **breath of consciousness**, your moral compass was activated.

That is the **Adam within you**. That is the fire in your clay.

Chapter 15: The Womb Blueprint: Embryo to Adam — The Perfect Analogy

The Quran is a profound book that repeatedly invites human beings to observe their own creation. Among the most remarkable analogies it employs is the comparison between the development of the human embryo and the greater journey of humanity itself. In Chapter 15, we explore how the stages of embryonic development provide not only a biological blueprint but also a symbolic and logical parallel to the emergence of Adam and the conscious human being.

Quranic Emphasis on Womb and Stages

The Quran refers several times to the stages of human creation in the womb:

> "We created man from an extract of clay. Then We placed him as a drop in a secure place. Then We made the drop into a clinging substance, and We made the clinging substance into a lump, and We made the lump into bones, and We clothed the bones with flesh; then We developed him into another creation. So blessed is Allah, the best of creators." (Quran 23:12-14)

This passage outlines a step-by-step transformation: clay (teen), drop (nutfah), clinging clot ('alaqah), lump (mudghah), bones ('izam), flesh (lahm), and then "another creation" (khalqan akhar). Each term corresponds with observable phases of embryology but also holds metaphorical potential.

The "another creation" stage indicates something qualitatively different. It implies the emergence of self-awareness, consciousness, and rational faculties — the very traits associated with "Adam" as a conscious being.

The Microcosm and Macrocosm: A Reflective Pattern

Embryogenesis is not merely a biological phenomenon; it is a mirror to the history of life itself. Just as the embryo evolves through simple to complex forms, the human species also progressed through evolutionary stages before reaching the conscious state represented by Adam.

The Quran invites us to look into ourselves:

> "And in yourselves, will you not then see?" (Quran 51:21)

This is not just an invitation to introspect, but to study our own physical and developmental reality as a map to understand deeper truths.

Scientific Basis: Embryo as Evolution in Micro-Time

Modern embryology confirms that in the early stages of development, human embryos exhibit features that resemble earlier evolutionary ancestors — gill-like structures, tail-like formations, and more. These features fade away or transform, but they show the retained memory of an evolutionary path. This process, called **ontogeny**, reflects **phylogeny** — the evolutionary history of species.

In this view, the womb becomes a compressed arena of evolution. What took millions of years in nature unfolds in weeks within the human mother's womb. This is not metaphorical poetry but a biological reality: we carry evolution within us.

Adam: The Emergence of Self-Aware Life

In the final stages of embryogenesis, the human fetus begins to display neural activity, memory responses, and post-birth potential for language and moral development. This echoes the Quranic notion that after the physical formation, a conscious spark is introduced:

> "Then He fashioned him and breathed into him from His Ruh (consciousness/spirit) ..." (Quran 32:9)

This verse does not speak of a magical or superstitious soul but refers to the activation of conscious selfhood — the arrival of awareness, reasoning, and will.

In this context, "Adam" is not a magically made man but the first being in whom this spark of self-aware ruh arose. The embryo becomes an analogy: from clay to a conscious being, just as from early organisms to Homo sapiens.

Linguistic Clues: From "Nutfah" to "Khalqan Akhar"

The Arabic term "khalqan akhar" — "another creation" — is of critical importance. It indicates a transition not merely of form but of existential nature. Before this stage, the embryo is a biological system. Afterward, it becomes a conscious being. Similarly, humanity before Adam was biologically evolving, but only with Adam came the rise of consciousness, morality, responsibility, and language.

The Quran uses terms that show intentional progression, not sudden supernatural events. The verb "ja'alna" (We made), "khalaqna" (We created), and "anfakhna" (We breathed) suggest a processual creation.

Philosophical Implication: The Womb as Revelation

The womb is not only a physical space but also a symbol of evolutionary continuity. The Quranic use of this analogy teaches us that the emergence of Adam — a conscious, moral, social human — is not disconnected from the laws of nature. It is deeply integrated into them.

This understanding dismantles the mythological view of creation as a one-time miraculous event and replaces it with a scientifically compatible, logically coherent process rooted in natural law.

Conclusion: Adam Reborn in Every Womb

Every human embryo reenacts the journey of Adam. Every fetus goes from clay-based chemistry to a conscious being. The miracle is not in violating nature but in following its perfect design.

Thus, Adam is not a myth. He is a milestone. He is not just the past; he is a pattern. The womb is not just a place of birth; it is the theater of nature's greatest transformation — from lifeless elements to a being who can name, imagine, question, and choose.

Understanding this analogy liberates the narrative of Adam from superstition and connects it to science, reason, and the divine system of evolution and consciousness. It is in the womb that both biology and destiny meet — where clay meets ruh, and nature meets purpose.

Chapter 16: The Fallacy of First Marriage – Is Incest in the Quran?

One of the most misunderstood and misrepresented stories from the Adam narrative is the so-called "first marriage" — the idea that Adam and Hawwa's (Eve's) children married each other (siblings marrying siblings) to populate the earth. This notion is widely circulated among traditional religious teachings, yet it is not explicitly mentioned anywhere in the Quran. In this chapter, we will analyze this belief from Quranic, logical, ethical, and scientific perspectives. We will challenge the inherited myth of incest and demonstrate that attributing such practices to divine intention undermines both human dignity and the message of moral evolution embedded within the Quran.

The Myth of Sibling Marriage

Many Islamic, Judaic, and Christian traditions claim that Adam and Eve had sons and daughters who married each other — a supposed necessity for human propagation. But we must ask: **Does the Quran endorse this?** The answer is clearly **no.**

There is **no verse in the Quran** that states or even implies that Adam's sons married their sisters. The Quran mentions the story of two sons of Adam (Surah Al-Ma'idah 5:27), one of whom killed the other due to jealousy and rejection of a divine offering. However, **there is no mention of who they were supposed to marry**, nor any instruction from God suggesting that incest was part of the divine plan.

Scientific and Genetic Objections to Incest

Modern genetics clearly warns against incest. Marriages between close relatives lead to a **high risk of genetic disorders**, birth defects, and inherited diseases. The very idea that the earliest human civilization, under divine guidance, would begin with a practice known today to cause **biological degeneration**, contradicts the idea of divine wisdom and the Quran's emphasis on purity, balance (mīzān), and harmony in creation.

Moreover, evolutionary science tells us that **humankind did not begin from a single couple**, but from a **gene pool of early human populations** who gradually developed higher cognitive and social traits over tens of thousands of years. This fits far more coherently with the idea that Adam was **not a biological first man**, but a symbol of the rise of human consciousness, leadership, and moral awareness.

Quranic Language and Divine Silence

The Quran never uses the word "Hawwa" (Eve), nor does it mention the number of Adam's children, their names, or their marriages. This **silence is meaningful**.

The Quran repeatedly uses the term **"Bani Adam" (Children of Adam)** to refer to **humanity as a whole**, not to literal biological offspring. If sibling marriage was a requirement of divine will, the Quran would have directly addressed this issue, explained its necessity, and morally justified it. But instead, **it remains silent**, which is a **method of divine disapproval**.

The Prophet (PBUH) is instructed in the Quran not to follow the myths of earlier people:

"Those are stories of the past; some of them We made clear to you, and some We did not..." (Surah Ghafir 40:78).

This verse indicates that **not all stories are repeated or endorsed**, especially if they serve no divine purpose or promote unethical ideas.

The Ethical Dimension: A Merciful God and Human Dignity

Would a just and wise Creator begin humanity's journey by promoting incest — a practice that even animals instinctively avoid? This would contradict the Quran's repeated themes of **tazkiyah (purification), fitrah (natural inclination), and hurmat (sacred boundaries)**.

The Quran says:

"Indeed, We have honored the children of Adam..."

(Surah Al-Isra 17:70)

This honor and dignity would not begin with a practice that humanity now universally rejects. The Quran's ethics are timeless, and any action that is ethically repulsive in modern society **cannot be claimed to be divinely mandated** in the past. Truth must remain constant across time, not bend to the myths of earlier cultures.

Where Did the Idea Come From?

The belief in incest as the first marriage is not from the Quran but from **Biblical and Talmudic narratives** and later **Islamic folklore**. Jewish and Christian texts introduced the idea that Adam and Eve's children (Cain and Abel) married their sisters. Later Islamic commentators — often influenced by Israelite traditions (**Isra'iliyyat**) — imported this idea into Islamic literature. However, this **has no basis in the Quran**, which explicitly warns against following conjecture:

"They follow nothing but conjecture, and indeed, conjecture can never substitute for the truth."

(Surah An-Najm 53:28)

Thus, repeating such myths under the name of Islam is a violation of the Quran's truth-centric approach.

Alternative Quranic Perspective: Adam as a Prototype

The Quran portrays Adam as the **symbol of human consciousness, freedom, and accountability**. He is a **khalifa** (vicegerent), not merely a biological father. His "children" represent the rise of human civilization, not a literal small family unit.

Human populations, according to evolutionary biology and archaeological findings, developed across different regions. The Quran supports this idea of **diverse human origin**:

"O mankind! We created you from a male and a female and made you peoples and tribes that you may know one another."

(Surah Al-Hujurat 49:13)

This verse doesn't point to a single family marrying each other, but rather to a **plurality of peoples** created for mutual understanding and peaceful coexistence. It affirms both **biological diversity** and **social structure**, not incest-based propagation.

Conclusion: Clearing the Dirt of Folklore

The myth of incest among Adam's children is **not a divine truth but a cultural fiction**, carried into Islamic tradition from other sources. The Quran's silence, the genetic impossibility, the ethical violation, and the message of human honor all point to one conclusion:

Humanity did not begin with incest.

Adam symbolizes the rise of conscious, moral, and intelligent beings — the beginning of **ethical civilization**, not **tribal taboo**. As students of both science and revelation, we must now move beyond myth, and restore the dignity of the Quran's message by rejecting inherited fictions and upholding the logic, ethics, and truth that the Quran itself champions.

Chapter 17: What the Quran Didn't Say — Silence as a Source of Clarity

One of the most neglected methods of Quranic interpretation is paying close attention to what the Quran *doesn't* say. While many religious narratives are filled with detailed stories, the Quran often omits these details. This silence is not a gap, but a method of instruction. When the Quran chooses not to speak about something, it forces the reader to question inherited interpretations, resist mythological interpolations, and confront the truth with reason.

This chapter explores what the Quran omits about the story of Adam, specifically in relation to Hawwa (Eve), the concept of incest, and other commonly assumed elements in Abrahamic traditions. Through a close analysis, we will understand how silence in the Quran is not an absence of guidance, but a form of higher communication that respects human reason and invites conscious reflection.

Absence of Hawwa (Eve) by Name

Most people assume that Hawwa (Eve) is a central character in the Quranic story of Adam. However, nowhere in the Quran is she mentioned by name. This is in sharp contrast to the Biblical narrative in Genesis.

Implication: The absence of her name indicates that the Quran is not concerned with personalizing the story of the "first woman." The focus is instead on the collective human experience of consciousness, responsibility, and choice. The dialogue is always between "Adam" and his Lord, and references like "you both" (dual form in Arabic) are gender-neutral.

This linguistic choice prevents the mythologization of Eve as the one who seduced or caused Adam to err. Unlike in Genesis, the Quran never blames the woman. Instead, both are held equally accountable. The Quran's silence on naming Eve protects the story from gender bias and theological sexism.

No Mention of First Children or Marriages

Another assumption often injected into the Quranic story is that Adam and Hawwa had sons and daughters who married each other. Inherited tales from Biblical and Hadith traditions claim that their children practiced intra-family marriages (incest) to begin the human race.

Quranic Position: The Quran is completely silent on this. It does not mention any such marriages. It does not say that Adam's children married their siblings, nor does it even tell us how humanity proliferated from the first pair.

Why This Silence Matters: Silence on this matter protects the Quran from moral contradictions. It avoids normalizing incest, which is condemned across cultures and also addressed later in Islamic ethics. Had the Quran mentioned such a practice, it would raise severe ethical and psychological questions.

Instead, by not detailing the process, the Quran encourages humans to explore biological and sociological possibilities without being forced to accept a morally problematic myth. This opens the door for understanding human origins through genetics, evolution, and anthropological study.

The Danger of Filling the Gaps with Folklore

Because of the Quran's minimalism in narrative, many scholars throughout history filled these gaps with Biblical and Isra'iliyyat (Judeo-Christian) traditions. These include stories of the Devil's physical rebellion, the fall of Adam from Heaven to Sri Lanka, and Eve being created from Adam's rib.

Scientific and Logical Problems:

- The rib story contradicts embryological development.
- The descent from Heaven as a physical fall contradicts the metaphorical intent of "Jannah."
- Assigning names and family trees creates a pseudo-history that cannot be verified.

The Quran deliberately resists these mythological additions. Its simplicity is intentional. Its silence on these tales is not oversight—it is resistance.

Silence as Respect for Human Intelligence

By remaining silent on speculative details, the Quran empowers human beings to reflect, question, and seek knowledge. It doesn't present ready-made stories to satisfy curiosity; instead, it offers ethical direction and moral principles.

For instance:

- The Quran does not tell us exactly what fruit was eaten.
- It does not tell us the names of Adam's children.
- It does not tell us how many years they lived or where they were buried.

Why? Because such information does not serve moral, spiritual, or intellectual growth. It would reduce the Quran to a book of myths. Instead, it directs our attention to values like accountability, reasoning, ego, decision-making, and social consciousness.

Methodology of Reading the Quran

To understand the purpose behind Quranic silence, we must adopt a new methodology:

- **Focus on what is said and why.**
- **Reflect on what is omitted and why.**
- **Avoid importing stories from external traditions without verification.**
- **Engage with the Quran using reason and cross-disciplinary knowledge.**

This approach reveals the Quran as a book of *huda* (guidance), not *qasas* (tales). It is not interested in satisfying curiosity but in awakening consciousness.

Conclusion

The Quran's silence is not a flaw—it is a doorway. In its refusal to indulge in unnecessary detail, it pushes the reader to rise above myth, avoid dogma, and pursue truth with intellect and sincerity. It prevents the hijacking of divine guidance by storytellers, sectarians, and sensationalists.

When we stop filling in the blanks with fiction, we begin to see the light that shines through the spaces. The story of Adam, in the Quran, is not a historical tale but a symbolic blueprint for the awakening of humanity. What the Quran didn't say often teaches us more than what it did.

Chapter 18: Scientific Translation of Misunderstood Terms — Ruh, Jannat, Shaitaan, Qalb

In this chapter, we reinterpret four Quranic terms that have often been misrepresented in religious discourse: *Ruh* (روح), *Jannat* (جنة), *Shaitaan* (شيطان), and *Qalb* (قلب). These terms are traditionally understood through mythological, mystical, or supernatural lenses. However, when examined in the light of language, science, and reason, they unfold a profound psychological, neurological, and ethical paradigm.

RUH (روح): Conscious Energy, not a Floating Soul

Traditional interpretation often equates *Ruh* with a supernatural soul—something that enters a body and exits upon death. But a linguistic and contextual analysis reveals a more scientific concept.

The Quran says:

> "They ask you concerning the Ruh. Say: The Ruh is by the command of my Lord, and you have been given of knowledge but little." (Quran 17:85)

The term *Amr-e-Rab* (command of your Lord) is key here. In Quranic usage, *Amr* signifies a system or law (like in 30:30 – "No change is there in the law of Allah"). Hence, *Ruh* refers to a law-bound phenomenon, not a mysterious entity.

Modern neuroscience points to consciousness as the highest expression of human identity. It's not a 'thing' but a process—a dynamic emergence from brain activity. *Ruh* can thus be understood as the system of consciousness, governed by divine law, emerging from within the biological vessel as a result of its complex neural evolution.

In this light, the *Ruh* is not an injected foreign entity but a reference to the human capacity for self-awareness, volition, and morality.

JANNAT (جنة): A Social and Psychological State, not a Physical Paradise

In popular religious thought, *Jannat* is portrayed as a post-death paradise with rivers of milk and wine, eternal pleasures, and physical luxuries. But this interpretation reduces the Quran's profound guidance to a bribe-based theology.

The word *Jannat* comes from the root ج ن ن, which means 'to cover' or 'to shield.' The same root is used in *jinn* (hidden beings), *janin* (fetus), and *majnoon* (one whose intellect is veiled).

In many Quranic verses, *Jannat* is described in allegorical terms:

> "Race toward forgiveness from your Lord and a Garden as wide as the heavens and the earth, prepared for the righteous." (Quran 3:133)

A garden as vast as the cosmos cannot be a literal field. It is a metaphor for a higher state of being—where justice, peace, and freedom prevail.

In the story of Adam, *Jannat* is a state where he lived free from hunger, thirst, and insecurity (Quran 20:118-119). Once ego, impulsive desire, or 'Shaitaan' led him to disobedience, he 'descended'—not physically but psychologically—from a state of harmony to one of struggle.

Hence, *Jannat* is a symbolic state of social and moral elevation—where humanity aligns with divine values. It is achieved through ethical living, not merely believed into existence. The post-death *Jannat* described in the Quran, too, is a continuation of this state, not a fantastical reward, but a reality formed by one's deeds and inner evolution.

SHAITAAN (شيطان): Instinctual Ego, not a Mythical Devil

The Quran defines *Shaitaan* not as a horned figure but as an adversarial tendency:

> "Surely, Shaitaan is your enemy, so take him as an enemy." (Quran 35:6)

The root of *Shaitaan* is *sha-ta-na*, meaning 'to separate' or 'to cause disharmony.' In the Quran, *Shaitaan* whispers, incites, and deceives. This aligns with what we now understand as ego-driven impulses—the internal forces of selfishness, arrogance, denial of truth, and instant gratification.

In psychology, this aligns with the limbic system—the primitive part of the brain associated with instinct, aggression, and impulse. It opposes the prefrontal cortex, which governs reason, foresight, and ethics.

So, *Shaitaan* is a symbolic representation of the lower self—biologically and psychologically ingrained instincts that, if unregulated, oppose the path of reason and moral consciousness.

QALB (قلب): The Mind's Dynamic Center, not a Beating Heart

In Arabic, *Qalb* literally means 'to turn' or 'to transform.' In the Quran, it is the seat of understanding, intention, and choice—not emotion:

> "They have hearts (Qulub) with which they do not understand." (Quran 7:179)

This shows that *Qalb* is not an emotional heart but a cognitive center. Modern science confirms that decision-making, judgment, and emotion regulation happen in the brain—particularly the prefrontal cortex, insula, and anterior cingulate cortex.

Thus, *Qalb* is the Quranic term for the dynamic, inner faculty of perception and reflection. It is where ethical battles are fought between *Shaitaan* (instinct) and *Ruh* (conscious awareness).

Conclusion: Reclaiming the Language of Revelation

These four terms—*Ruh*, *Jannat*, *Shaitaan*, and *Qalb*—are not magical abstractions but scientifically and ethically significant concepts. They map a sophisticated human psychology, rooted in reason, responsibility, and higher consciousness.

By stripping away superstition and reclaiming the Quranic language in light of neuroscience and moral philosophy, we return to the core message: that humans are not puppets of fate or recipients of myth, but architects of their own transformation.

Chapter 19: Religion vs Revelation – How Scholars Betrayed Adam

From Divine Revelation to Doctrinal Corruption

The Quran presents itself as *Hudan li-nnaas* (guidance for humanity), a living message that awakens the human mind and heart. It was never introduced as a system of rituals or clergy-led dogma. Yet over centuries, the essence of this revelation—meant to liberate, enlighten, and elevate—was systematically replaced by organized religious structures, political tafsirs, and scholar-imposed doctrines.

Among the biggest victims of this betrayal is the story of **Adam**. The original Quranic portrayal of Adam is vastly different from the fairy-tale version promoted by traditional religious scholars. This chapter will expose how religious authorities twisted the Quranic text, invented details not found in revelation, and suppressed interpretations that align with logic, science, and moral responsibility.

The Political Roots of Traditional Tafsir

After the death of Prophet Muhammad, the caliphates and dynasties that followed quickly realized the power of religion as a tool for control. To maintain political authority, rulers patronized scholars and jurists who could provide religious legitimacy to their regimes. Tafsir (Quranic interpretation) was no longer a matter of sincere understanding—it became a political enterprise.

In this environment, the story of Adam was turned into a literalist myth:

- Adam was declared the *first human being*, created instantly out of clay.
- Hawwa (Eve), said to be created from his rib, was introduced as the origin of women.
- The concept of original sin entered Islamic thought, influenced by

Jewish and Christian ideas.
- The descent from paradise became a tale of punishment, rather than a metaphor of consciousness.

None of these details are explicitly mentioned in the Quran.

The Myth of Literalism: Adam as a Man, not a Metaphor

Traditional interpretations insist that Adam was a single man, and all humans are his biological descendants. However, the Quran never claims this directly.

Quranic language allows Adam to be interpreted:

- As a **prototype of moral consciousness**.
- As a **collective symbol** of early humankind.
- As a **metaphor** for the rise of decision-making, free will, and societal responsibility.

The moment we reduce Adam to a literal figure in a garden with a wife and an apple, we shut the door on rational exploration. Scholars chose this path to align with the Biblical narrative and pacify the public with familiar stories.

Inventing What the Quran Never Said

Here are major elements that **scholars added** to the Adam story—none of which exist in the Quran:

- **Hawwa (Eve)**: Her name does not appear even once in the Quran.
- **Creation from a Rib**: This idea comes from Hadith literature and Jewish traditions—not the Quran.
- **Snake or Devil in the Tree**: No serpent or talking animal is mentioned.
- **Original Sin and Human Guilt**: The Quran absolves Adam through repentance (Surah 2:37), and does not transmit sin to humanity.
- **Earth as a punishment**: Nowhere does the Quran say Adam was "thrown to Earth" as a penalty. Earth is always the intended phase for

moral development.

These additions did not clarify the text—they corrupted it. They converted a profound psychological, social, and moral parable into a fantasy.

Shifting from Revelation to Ritual

Once religious scholars took control of interpretation, they shifted focus away from Quranic reasoning to ritualistic obedience. They:

- Turned *Salat* (connection, engagement) into a rigid performance.
- Turned *Zakat* (purification of self and society) into a tax percentage.
- Turned *Ruh* (conscious energy) into a mysterious ghost-like soul.
- And turned Adam's lesson of free will into a deterministic sin-story.

This same pattern applied to the story of Adam. Instead of extracting lessons about ego, choice, social responsibility, and moral consciousness, scholars focused on justifying rituals and rules based on an invented fall from grace.

Suppressing Scientific and Rational Voices

Throughout Islamic history, several thinkers—like Ibn Sina, Al-Farabi, and later thinkers like Muhammad Iqbal—tried to bring back a philosophical and rational interpretation of Adam and creation. They interpreted *clay*, *breath*, and *names* as symbolic stages of consciousness, not literal events.

But these voices were suppressed. The dominant religious elite branded them as heretics, silencing the possibility of scientific and philosophical engagement with the Quran. This was not just a betrayal of Adam—it was a betrayal of the Quran's call to think, reflect, and reason.

The Scholar as the New Pharaoh

Ironically, the very scholars who claimed to uphold religion became the modern equivalent of the Pharaohs condemned in the Quran:

- They demanded obedience without evidence.

- They claimed exclusive authority over interpretation.
- They feared loss of power if people began to think independently.

The Quran warns against such figures repeatedly:

> *"They have taken their scholars and monks as lords besides Allah..."*
>
> (Surah At-Tawbah 9:31)

This is not a warning against spirituality—it's a warning against the **monopolization of truth** by self-proclaimed interpreters.

7. Reclaiming the True Adam: Mind Over Myth

To restore Adam's dignity, we must return to the Quran itself:

- **Clay (Teen)** represents our biochemical origin—carbon-based life.
- **Breath of Ruh** symbolizes the emergence of consciousness and free will.
- **Teaching of names** signifies the rise of memory, language, and cognition.
- **Tree and forbidden fruit** reflect the challenge of ethical responsibility.
- **Descent from Jannat** is not about location but about maturity—the shift from innocence to accountability.

These elements are not myths—they are **scientific, psychological, and spiritual realities** dressed in metaphor. Adam is not just history—Adam is every one of us when we become aware of our power to choose.

Conclusion: From Betrayal to Awakening

The story of Adam in the Quran was meant to be an eternal lesson—not a bedtime story. It was meant to awaken the mind, not suppress it. Scholars, under pressure from politics and tradition, chose the path of betrayal.

But the Quran is still accessible. Its language still calls out to the rational, moral, and conscious being in all of us. By revisiting Adam through the lenses of **science**, **psychology**, and **linguistic truth**, we do not reject revelation—we fulfill its original mission.

Chapter 20: Reclaiming Adam – A New Beginning for Humanity

Restoring the True Meaning of the First Conscious Being

Why We Must Reclaim Adam

In the previous chapter, we exposed how religious authorities corrupted the original message of Adam in the Quran. They converted a dynamic, symbolic narrative into a frozen myth. Now, in this final chapter, we aim to reclaim the real Adam—not just as an individual of the past, but as the first awakening of consciousness, ethics, and human responsibility.

To reclaim Adam means to reclaim ourselves—our intellect, our choices, and our place in the universe. The Quran offers a revolutionary perspective on Adam that aligns with modern science, psychology, and moral philosophy. This chapter restores that vision, point by point.

Adam Is Not the First Man—He Is the First Conscious Being

The Quran never says "Adam was the first human." What it shows instead is:

- Adam was *taught names* (Surah Al-Baqarah 2:31), implying **language, classification, memory, and consciousness**.
- Adam had **free will**—he made a choice and bore its consequences.
- Adam was given **divine potential** but was not forced—he had to activate it by self-awareness.

This tells us that "Adam" is not necessarily a name for a male individual, but **a representation of the first stage in human evolution where the species gained conscious thought, moral understanding, and decision-making ability**.

This is supported by science: Homo sapiens as a species may be around 300,000 years old, but evidence of **symbolic thinking, ethical behavior, and abstract**

reasoning—what we might call "Adam-level consciousness"—appears more recently in archaeological records.

The Real Meaning of Jannat (Paradise)

Traditional interpretations turn Jannat into a physical garden somewhere in the skies. But the Quranic language allows for a more coherent, scientific interpretation:

- *Jannat* in Arabic means **a hidden or protected state**—like a womb, or a safe space.
- Adam's "Jannat" was not a literal garden with talking animals, but a **symbolic phase** where he lived in innocence and lack of responsibility.
- The *tree* he was told to avoid represents the **freedom to choose**—the emergence of **consequence-based ethics**.

The moment Adam chose to eat from the tree, it marks the **transition from instinct to awareness**. This is not a fall, but an **evolution**. It's not about divine punishment—it's about the birth of **moral responsibility**.

Just as a child must leave the womb to grow, Adam had to step out of that protected Jannat and face the world with free will and accountability. Jannat is not a punishment to be lost—it is a **state of mind** we strive to regain through moral consciousness.

The Role of Shaitaan (Satan) in the Story

In traditional stories, Shaitaan is a cartoon villain who tricks Adam. But the Quran gives a far more sophisticated view.

Shaitaan in the Quran:

- Was not an external evil demon, but a **symbol of arrogance, ego, and resistance to truth**.
- Refused to bow to Adam not out of theological disagreement, but

due to **pride and racial/elemental superiority**: "I am better than him. You made me from fire and him from clay." (Surah Al-A'raf 7:12)

This is a psychological truth. The "Shaitaan" is within us—it is our **inflated ego**, our refusal to accept equality, our desire to dominate. The Quran says: *"He whispers in the breasts of mankind"* (Surah An-Naas), showing that Satan is not an outer force, but an **inner tendency**.

So, Adam's encounter with Shaitaan was not about a supernatural being—it was about the first internal battle between **ego and humility**, between **impulse and reason**.

Qalb – The Heart-Mind Center

The Quran consistently speaks of *Qalb* as the place of understanding, insight, and transformation. This does not refer to the physical heart, but to the **core of consciousness and decision-making**.

The real story of Adam involves this *Qalb*—his **emotional and mental center** that allows him to:

- Recognize right from wrong
- Feel regret and guilt
- Accept divine guidance
- Transform himself after failure

The moment Adam feels regret (*fa taaba alaihi*, Surah 2:37), he demonstrates **emotional intelligence**. This is the *Qalb*—not heart in the biological sense, but the **neural-emotional network** that allows us to reflect, feel, and act with wisdom.

Adam's evolution was not physical. It was **neuro-psychological**. He became "human" the moment he could process emotion, reflect on failure, and seek a higher truth.

The Rise of Responsibility, Not Sin

The most revolutionary part of the Adam story in the Quran is this:

- Adam is not blamed eternally for his mistake.
- He is not cursed or banished in rage.
- He is **guided** and given another chance.

"Then his Lord chose him, and turned to him with forgiveness, and gave him guidance."

(Surah Taha 20:122)

This shows the core difference between the Quran and religious mythology:

- In religion, man is fallen and sinful.
- In revelation, man is *capable, evolving, and guided.*

Adam's story is the first **lesson of human freedom, error, and recovery**. He symbolizes not a curse, but a **calling**—a call to rise above base instincts and become a conscious contributor to the universe.

Reclaiming Adam Means Reclaiming Ourselves

The Quran tells us:

> *"We have certainly honored the children of Adam..."*
>
> (Surah Al-Isra 17:70)

This is not about race, bloodline, or nationality. It's about **conscious evolution.** The real "children of Adam" are those who:

- Use their *Qalb* to reflect and feel.
- Resist the inner Shaitaan of arrogance and ego.
- Strive to re-enter a state of Jannat—not through rituals, but through **ethical life and consciousness**.

Reclaiming Adam means:

- Understanding our true potential.
- Challenging religious dogma with rational, moral insight.
- Reconnecting with the original Quranic message: **"Read" (Iqra)—reflect, explore, awaken.**

Final Conclusion: A New Beginning for Humanity

The Quran did not come to create a new religion. It came to awaken the **inherent potential** within the human being. The story of Adam, when freed from religious corruption, becomes a **scientific, psychological, and moral map** of our species' evolution.

We are all Adam. And we all fall. But like him, we are capable of rising—through reflection, connection, and moral growth.

Religion tried to trap Adam in a myth.

Revelation sets him—and us—free.

Final Message to the Reader

Dear Reader,

As you close the final chapter of this journey, know that this book was never meant to offer all the answers—but to awaken the courage to ask better questions.

The story of Adam is not buried in ancient dust or confined to distant mythology. It lives within you—in your conscience, your reason, your choices, and your evolving sense of self. You are part of this conscious lineage, not by inheritance of blood, but by inheritance of thought. To be "Adam" is to rise above instinct, question-imposed dogmas, and embody moral intelligence in an age darkened by both superstition and arrogance.

If this book has inspired you to see the Quran not as a tool of ritual, but as a manifesto of awakening—then it has fulfilled its purpose. If it has urged you to reclaim your mind from the grip of blind tradition, and reconnect with the divine system through reason, justice, and empathy—then the story of Adam continues in you.

This is not the end. It is a beginning.

Let your life be the next verse.

– Harsa Khan

Author & Researcher

May 2025

Did you love *The Conscious Evolution: Reinterpreting Adam Through Science and Revelation*? Then you should read *BANI ISRAEL: IDEOLOGY, NOT INHERITANCE*[1] by Harsa khan!

[2]

This book is not the product of academic privilege, inherited tradition, or religious conformity. It is born from a deep yearning for truth — raw, unfiltered, and rooted in the Quran itself. For too long, the identity of Bani Israel has been defined by race, lineage, and external scriptures. But the Quran tells a different story — one that speaks of ideology, not inheritance. One that calls humanity not toward tribal superiority, but toward moral responsibility.

This work is the result of years of personal study, introspection, and repeated confrontation with the disconnect between traditional interpretations and the Quranic text. I have come to see Bani Israel not as a historical nation tied to a bloodline, but as a timeless group: those entrusted with knowledge, burdened with reform, and tested by power. Sometimes they rise; often they fail — but they are not alone. Every age has its own Bani Israel.

1. https://books2read.com/u/bwEqY9

2. https://books2read.com/u/bwEqY9

This book does not offer easy conclusions. It invites you to question — not just the narratives you've inherited, but the assumptions that underpin your worldview. It re-centers the Quran as the ultimate lens through which we must view identity, guidance, and responsibility. In these pages, you'll find a call to return — not to a race or ritual — but to the original mission given to Adam, carried forward by Nuh, and embodied by Ibrahim: the mission to build a just, conscious, and awakened society.

If this book shakes your comfort, good. If it awakens your heart, better. And if it empowers you to carry the ark of thought through the flood of confusion — then it has served its purpose.

Also by Harsa khan

BANI ISRAEL: IDEOLOGY, NOT INHERITANCE
Decoding Masr: Quran, Civilization and Historical Distortion
The Conscious Evolution: Reinterpreting Adam Through Science and Revelation
From Enlightenment to Empire: The Fall of Islam's Golden

9 789334 308907

Printed at Repro India Ltd.